THE LETTERS OF
JOHN GAY

Oxford University Press, Ely House, London W. 1

GLASGOW NEW YORK TORONTO MELBOURNE WELLINGTON
CAPE TOWN SALISBURY IBADAN NAIROBI LUSAKA ADDIS ABABA
BOMBAY CALCUTTA MADRAS KARACHI LAHORE DACCA
KUALA LUMPUR HONG KONG TOKYO

JOHN GAY

From an engraving by Francis Kyte after a portrait by William Aikman
('Mrs. Howard's painting')

THE LETTERS

OF

JOHN GAY

EDITED BY

C. F. BURGESS

OXFORD

AT THE CLARENDON PRESS

1966

To

JOHN TOWNER FREDERICK

with gratitude

CONTENTS

THE LETTERS

Contents

Contents

Contents

x

INTRODUCTION

IN pursuing a research project a few years ago, which called for extensive reference to the letters of John Gay, the editor arrived at three convictions: that Gay's letters needed to be brought together and considered as an entity; that the published versions of many of the letters contained sufficient editorial inconsistencies and textual errors to warrant their republication; that an intensive and systematic search would turn up an appreciable number of unpublished letters. These convictions prompted the present volume.

Time, the great disseminator, has worked particular havoc with Gay's correspondence. His letters are widely and indiscriminately scattered, with nothing resembling a representative body in any one place. They are to be found in various editions of eighteenth-century correspondence—here and there in Ball's *The Correspondence of Jonathan Swift, D.D.*, in Sherburn's *The Correspondence of Alexander Pope*, in the 1737 and 1740 editions of Pope's letters, in Croker's *Suffolk Correspondence* (out of print for nearly a century and a half), as miscellaneous material in Nichol Smith's *Letters from Jonathan Swift to Charles Ford*, in Warner's *Original Letters* (also many years out of print), and the list is not yet exhausted. Other letters appear as appendix items in editions of Gay's *Works* or are inserted at random in the introduction, and still others are in scholarly journals where they were published as they were discovered. Under these conditions, the search for a particular letter, unless accompanied by incredible luck, is a task of major proportions; and reading all of the letters, a monumental one. In these circumstances, the editor readily persuaded himself that the project which had brought him to the letters originally was of lesser import than that of undertaking to bring order to the epistolary chaos which confronted him.

To begin with, then, this volume seeks to provide a convenient, single source for all of Gay's letters now known to be extant. Letters *to* Gay have been excluded since accurate texts of the bulk of these, especially the letters from Pope and Swift, are now available in the Sherburn edition of Pope's correspondence and Sir Harold Williams's edition of Swift's correspondence.

Multiple editorship has contributed further to the chaotic state of Gay's letters. The published versions now available range in quality from eminently accurate and faithful transcripts, to what must be called, in all generosity, individual interpretations. It is something of an editorial commonplace that letters can generally be treated in one of two ways: as historical documents, in which case, *literatim* readings are called for; or, as types of literature, in which case, modernization of spelling and syntax for ease in reading is warranted. Gay's letters have been subjected to both historical and literary treatment, as well as curious amalgams of these two approaches. Many are reproduced with scrupulous accuracy, exactly as Gay wrote them; many have been edited to conform to modern writing practices; and many have appeared in print, at once both fish and fowl, in which present-day syntax and punctuation are introduced, while the vagaries of eighteenth-century spelling and orthography ('ye' for 'the', raised letters, contractions) are unaccountably retained.

In this edition, consistency of treatment and accuracy of reading are the desiderata, and to these ends the editor has endeavoured to present, with minor exceptions to be noted, what Gay wrote in the way he wrote. This may, at times, pose difficulties for the reader. He may occasionally find himself bewildered by a sentence or a passage, especially in the portions of the joint letters written by the Duchess of Queensberry, whose notions of grammar, punctuation, and spelling were, to be gallant, peculiar to herself. The editor submits, however, that this is the lesser evil. Once alterations by way of modernization are made, it becomes difficult to decide where to draw the line. The alternative to unremitting consistency is the chaos in the handling of the letters which has existed.

In the interest of accuracy, several steps have been taken.

If the original letter is still extant, the transcript has been made either from the original or from a photocopy or microfilm of the original. In the course of preparing this text all known Gay autographs have been located, an undertaking which involved much literary detective work, considerable travel, and a staggering amount of correspondence. In the case of letters which are known only from printed versions, the transcripts were taken from the texts where the letters were first published. Finally, both the typescript and the proofs have been read with painstaking care.

The editor's third conviction proved to be ill-founded. Despite a conscientious and exhaustive search, only one unpublished letter, Gay to the Countess of Burlington, 28 August 1726 (No. 39), has come to light. One other letter, Gay to Charles Ford, 27 June 1714 (No. 9), known in part but missing since 1896, was located again. The two miscellaneous items in the Appendix, although previously unpublished, have been known to earlier scholars.

This dearth of new material would seem to lead to one of two conclusions: that Gay wrote relatively few letters, or that time has again done Gay a disservice, in this instance aided and abetted by careless hands through which his letters have passed. Actually, there is evidence to justify both of these conclusions.

Gay is traditionally considered to have been an altogether charming, witty, and accomplished, but somewhat sporadic, letter writer. It is certainly true that compared to the voluminous correspondence of Chesterfield or Walpole or even Pope and Swift, Gay's efforts in this direction were modest. Two factors limited Gay's output. In the first place, he disliked writing letters, as he freely confessed in a letter to Thomas Parnell, April–May 1714 (No. 6). The same reluctance to discipline himself which sometimes made it difficult for him to work, apparently also applied in his correspondence. For Gay, it was so much easier to talk: 'I have ten thousand things to talk to you but few to write . . .', he told Swift in one of his letters to his friend and mentor in Ireland. To the gregarious and extroverted Gay, letters were a poor substitute for the joy of being surrounded by, and conversing with, his friends. 'The next pleasure to seeing of you is hearing from you . . .', he wrote to Mrs. Howard; and in order to enjoy this chief pleasure he was constantly urging his friends to come and see him or making plans to visit them. Secondly, Gay was, more often than not, so engaged in the role of 'Augustan Peter Pan' which James R. Sutherland has assigned him, so busy being 'always upon the ramble' to Bath, to Tunbridge, to Wiltshire, to Oxfordshire, that he scarcely had time for extensive correspondence. Swift protested that, since Gay was 'sometimes in Scotland, sometimes at Ham Walks, sometimes God knows where', he was forced to 'write at' him for lack of knowing where to 'write to' him. Moreover, even when Gay did sit down to write, he was apparently seldom able to write at length without being interrupted by the demands of his numerous social obligations. There is a feeling almost of breathlessness in many of Gay's letters and of an urgency to be finished writing. 'Just this minute', he frequently reports in the course of a letter, someone has come into the room or he has been invited to go on an excursion and must break off.

Yet, withal, strangely enough it was Gay who often complained that the Post had disappointed him, that his correspondents had deserted him. And, significantly, his correspondents (Swift included, who at one time owed Gay a letter for nearly a year) did not gainsay him. The chief complaint, in fact, which his correspondents raised was not that Gay was remiss in writing but that, like Swift, they were at a loss to know where to direct to him. What appears to be the truth is that Gay's circle of correspondents was rather limited, but within that circle he was reasonably faithful and diligent as a letter writer.

Had Gay's letters been preserved with the care accorded many of the eighteenth-century letter writers, this diligence would no doubt be attested to. There is, of course, no way of knowing how many of Gay's letters have been lost, but presumptive evidence indicates that the number is considerable. There were, for instance, letters to Lord Warwick, to William Fortescue, to Molly Lepell, to the Duchess of Hamilton, to Chesterfield, to Mary Bellenden, several to Pope and Swift and Mrs. Howard, all of them documented by contemporary references and all of them now missing. So too, the single new letter which was discovered during the preparation of this volume provokes speculation that it was only one of many. Gay was an intimate and a favourite in the Burlington household for some fifteen years and it is scarcely to be credited that he wrote but one letter to his friends and patrons, the Burlingtons, during this period. Finally, there is the persistent tradition of an exchange of letters between Gay and Allan Ramsay the Elder, growing out of the friendship formed between the two poets while Gay was in Edinburgh with the Queensberrys in 1729. The editor regretfully reports that the Gay–Ramsay correspondence remains a tradition, for the time being at least, having promised much but provided nothing.

THE JOHN GAY OF THE LETTERS

The letters offer no strikingly new insights, either into Gay the man or Gay the artist. Rather, they tend to substantiate the conventional portrait painted by Gay's contemporaries and brought into relief by scholars and critics in the two hundred years and more since his death.

The John Gay who emerges from his letters was first of all a man very much in love with life and the world about him, and at the same time a bit overwhelmed by what life and the world had to offer. Gay was scarcely of a philosophical bent, but he must on occasion have given thought to the kindly disposition of providence in granting him the talent for making poems and plays which had enabled a one-time linen draper's apprentice to become a companion and confidant of the great and the celebrated.

Life, in which such wonders could come to pass, was to be cherished. Gay's letters, accordingly, frequently convey his satisfaction at being alive to enjoy what the day has brought him; and, just as frequently, they are punctuated with expressions of concern for his own health and anxious inquiries after the well-being of his friends.

So too, the promising new world which good fortune and his poetic skills had opened up to him was to be cultivated. The evidence in the letters of Gay's efforts in this direction is sometimes painful to read. He wrote to Charles Ford from aboard the Channel vessel *Henrietta*, as he was about to sail for the Continent with 'My Lord Clarendon', and could not resist a postscript calling attention to his acquaintance with 'Lady Isabella', daughter of the Duchess of Monmouth; writing to his kinsman, William Fortescue, he took pains to let family and friends in Devonshire know that he had been 'a Shooting' with 'my Lord Essex' (who was not yet seventeen at the time); he addressed a letter to the Countess of Burlington in Paris that had nothing to say, but it served as a reminder that Mr. Gay was still 'Your Ladyship's & my Lord's' humble servant; he informed Pope that he was going to Hampton Court for a week where he would 'mix with Quality' and then managed to redeem the gaucherie by turning it into a compliment to his friend. Throughout the letters, but especially in the earlier ones, the great names whom Gay numbered among his acquaintances flow from his pen—Oxford, Bathurst, Burlington, the Duchesses of Monmouth and Marlborough, Queensberry—as do the names of the great estates where he mingled with them on easy footing—Dawley, Moor Park, Amesbury, Stanton Harcourt, Cassiobury—and Gay's elation at being able to write of them is quite evident.

The winds of fortune blew so favourably for Gay in this bright and brave world that he was early convinced that the grand prize which it had to offer—a place of consequence at Court—was attainable. In 1714 Princess Caroline of Anspach did the Secretary to the Clarendon Mission the honour of asking for a copy of *The Shepherd's Week* and Gay wrote in haste to Charles Ford for 'three or four' copies of this poem and a like number of *The Fan* to be sent to Hanover with the utmost dispatch. Gay was persuaded that the Princess's gesture was an entrée to the Court and that his success was assured. Political considerations, which govern the actions and shape the destinies of kings and ministers and courts, Gay overlooked completely or else they meant nothing to him. (Gay's political naïveté was almost total. In an age of strong party allegiances he professed not to care 'one Farthing' for a man's politics; and in an era in which an interest in politics was often a ruling passion his apathy toward political matters is remarkable. In the letters

Gay uses the words 'Whig' or 'Tory' only twice.) The grand prize ultimately eluded him, but for fourteen years Gay refused to believe it would not be his. When Princess Caroline, now Princess of Wales, came to England later in the same year, Gay was ready with a poetical reminder of his presence, and of his hopes. And there was still another reminder in 1727, *The Fables*, dedicated to the Duke of Cumberland, the Princess's son.

The world had much to offer Gay and had given him much. Artistic and social success had been his almost without his bidding. Finding the world apparently predisposed in his favour, Gay came to accept its tenets, to believe in its promises, and to expect much, perhaps too much. 'My Friends do a great deal for me,' he wrote to Francis Colman, 'but I think I could do more for them.' Writing to Swift, he reported that he had received 'many Civilitys from many great men but very few real benefits. They wonder at each other for not providing for me, and I wonder at 'em all.' It is abundantly clear that he had expected something more than the post of Gentleman-Usher which the Princess who had been kind to him in Hanover, now Queen Caroline, offered him in 1727. Given his background as fortune's favourite, Gay was unprepared for the revelation that the world was not always as brave and as bright as he envisioned it. His friends had tried to prepare him; Pope and Swift, and especially Mrs. Howard, who was only too well acquainted with the world with its tinsel and glitter removed, warned him in their letters not to set his hopes too high or expect too much. Gay gave all this good advice a careful hearing, and, in his replies, professed to have profited by it; but in the main he continued to believe only what he wanted to believe.

Gay's principal shortcoming, as a man and as an artist, was his lack of a sense of perspective. The world was simply too much with him and he was unable to take a detached and objective view of it. He was unable, despite his frequent protestations of indifference, to disabuse himself wholly of his view of the world as a place where dreams are realized and promises are kept. Indeed it would have been difficult for Gay to believe otherwise; his own life, everything that had happened to him, testified to the soundness of this view.

Ironically, the same idealism and measureless enthusiasm which rendered Gay ill-equipped to cope with the world were the ingredients of his success in living in the world. The two qualities account, in large part, for Gay's legendary personal charm, for the 'Honest' or 'Gentle' Gay whom his friends loved, over-trusting, generous to a fault, wearing his heart openly on his sleeve for all to see. The letters cast a good deal of light on this side of his character.

If we may accept the evidence of the letters, John Gay must have been a thoroughly delightful companion. By their testimony, he appears to have been interested in everything and everybody; nothing was of too little consequence to escape his discerning eye. He had, preeminently, a talent amounting to genius for remarking the trivia of life and he was always ready with a witty or provocative or graceful commentary, as the occasion demanded. If Gay talked as he wrote, if the common belief that letters in the eighteenth century were often another medium in which to practice the art of conversation is true, any gathering in which Gay was numbered must have been in continual high good humour.

Gay's charm comes through in other ways in the letters. Swift often scolded him and lectured him about his health and his finances, but only because his affection for Gay was boundless. Gay, in turn, took it all with good grace and, like the chastened schoolboy, promised to do better. Arbuthnot nursed him when he was sick, more as friend than physician, and Gay responded by writing to Swift that he was now indebted to Arbuthnot for his life. After the *Polly* affair, Swift, who had grown wise in courts, suspected Mrs. Howard, Gay's friend at Court, of having abandoned him, but Gay himself regretted only that he was now *persona non grata* and could not call on her as before. Gay's personal attractiveness is perhaps best summed up by the Duke of Queensberry in one of those asides which are more meaningful than reams of formal testimony. Writing to Swift, Queensberry, one of the most exalted of the Peers of the Realm, took evident satisfaction in being able to refer to the draper's apprentice turned poet as 'my friend John'.

But attractive as his simple faith in the world may have made him personally, this same quality was a material handicap to Gay the would-be satirist. Above all else, the satirist must be able to convince his audience that the folly he would expose is indeed folly. Hence he must be able to look upon his target dispassionately and without reservations, convinced that its destruction is for the greater good. As a breaker of idols Gay is notably indecisive; having struck the first blow, he then stands back to grieve over the damage. Throughout most of his career Gay was evidently never able to despise the world as Swift professed to do, and may indeed, have done, or to view it with philosophical detachment as Pope taught himself to do. As a result, the effectiveness of much of Gay's satire, as many critics have noted, is compromised by his inability to maintain the necessary aesthetic distance. In mounting the attack Gay has reservations; as a satirist he is often unconvinced and unconvincing.

Some of Gay's attempts at satire in the letters illustrate the difficulties he encountered in remaining sufficiently detached from his material. One of his lesser epistolary efforts is a long letter which he wrote to Swift on 16 August 1714 (No. 12) from the Hanoverian Court. In it he presented a burlesque manual or *vade mecum* for aspiring young diplomats. It is exceptional among Gay's letters in that it is tedious and dull. It represents Gay adopting the pose of the cynic, a role ill-suited to his nature, and the attempt at satire falls very flat. Perhaps Gay wrote it in order to demonstrate his equanimity amidst courts and princes and princesses. Perhaps he wrote it because he thought that this is what the tough-minded Dean expected from him. Or perhaps because this was an age of satire Gay felt that he must perforce be a satirist. In any event, Gay's primer for diplomats is top-heavy with laboured thrusts at the ways of a court and with the technical terms of statecraft with which Gay, the neophyte secretary, was becoming familiar. The fundamental reason for the satire's failure, however, is that the satirist himself so obviously takes it all rather seriously. Gay's overt delight in displaying his new-found acquaintance with the world of diplomacy, in using terms like 'Embassadors Extraordinary' and 'Plenipotentiarys' and 'Envoys in Ordinary', and his gratification at having been in the 'Presence of the Prince' at a 'Levee' soon overwhelm the joke.

Gay's inability to maintain aesthetic distance, his refusal to abandon his hopes and his faith in the world, are manifest elsewhere in the letters. Again and again he protests his indifference, his stoicism, in the face of disappointment. Indeed, he protests too much and his protestations recall Lessing's observation that men seldom speak of the virtues they have, but often of those they lack. In a letter to Mrs. Howard in August 1723 (No. 33), he philosophized wittily on the falseness of statesmen and courts and professed to be done with them for ever; yet two years later he abruptly interrupted a visit to the Queensberrys in Wiltshire in order to hurry back to London on receiving news that a place at Court might be available (Gay and Pope to Fortescue, 23 September 1725 (No. 36)). In a moment of temporary pique, or perhaps, 'fashionable indignation', to use another of Professor Sutherland's phrases, Gay informed Pope that he had come to realize that 'Life is a Jest' and the world he had been trying to cultivate, a barren place (October 1727 (No. 46)). But again, Gay is neither really convinced nor convincing. The psychic wound apparently healed without a trace of a scar, since within a few months (15 February 1727/8 (No. 49)) Gay was writing to Swift, with obvious satisfaction, of the success of *The Beggar's Opera* and of its acceptance by the world he had ostensibly rejected.

The fact that the *Polly* affair came scarcely a year after his disappointment at being offered the post of Gentleman-Usher might very well have shaken at last Gay's belief that the world and its works were essentially good. There is, in fact, some suggestion in the letters of this time that Gay did begin to question, and perhaps to doubt. On 2 December 1728 he expressed his bewilderment in a letter (No. 54) to Swift, over the furor *Polly* had caused: 'I am sure I have written nothing that can be legally supprest, unless the setting vices in general in an odious light, and virtue in an amiable one may give offence.' The ways of the world were as incomprehensible to Gay in 1728 as they had been in 1714.

But faith such as Gay's is rare enough to demand reward, and fortune does not readily abandon those it has decided to smile upon. In the midst of the crisis over *Polly*, just as Gay was starting to waver, he was given dramatic proof of the world's solicitude for its favourites. Gay's friends rallied to his cause, some, no doubt, for reasons of their own, but many more out of genuine affection for the beleaguered poet. 'Mrs. Howard', Gay wrote to Swift (18 March 1728/9 (No. 55)), 'hath declar'd herself strongly both to the King & Queen as my advocate.' The Duchess of Marlborough gave £100 for one copy of *Polly*. The Duchess's generosity was unique in its extent, but at the same time it was typical of the support Gay received. As a result, the subscriptions for the published version of *Polly* exceeded £1,200.

The world redeemed itself most convincingly, however, in the persons of the Duke and Duchess of Queensberry.

The ardour with which the Queensberrys defended him was particularly gratifying to Gay. For the Duke the suppression of *Polly* was the climactic move in a series of high-handed acts on the part of the Ministry, and to make clear his displeasure he relinquished his appointments and voluntarily exiled himself from the Court. The Duchess, the volatile and unpredictable Catherine Hyde, was especially solicitous on Gay's behalf and her efforts finally brought about her banishment from Court. Gay's gratitude to his two noble Samaritans was immediate and whole-hearted. The Queensberrys, Gay wrote to Swift (18 March 1728/9 (No. 55)), had treated him as if he had been 'their nearest relation and nearest friend', and he assured the Dean that he owed the Duchess his 'Life & fortune' (9 November 1729 (No. 58)).

The letters which Gay wrote during the last four years of his life, the years he spent largely with the Queensberrys, are pleasant to read. There is, to be sure, an occasional, tentative jibe at the ways of the world and an occasional hint of some disenchantment, as in this report to Swift (8 November 1730 (No. 65)) of his meeting Lord Carteret, lately dismissed as Lord-Lieutenant of Ireland: 'He seem'd to take to me, which I take to proceed from your recommendation; though indeed there is another reason for it, for he is now out of Employment, and my friends have generally been of that sort; for I take to them as being naturally inclin'd to those who can do no mischief.' On the whole, however, Gay's state of mind during the closing years of his life is probably more accurately summed up by his comment to

Swift (3 March 1729/30 (No. 59)): 'I dont hate the world
but I laugh at it.' Gay's success in laughing at the world is
a moot point but he assuredly had no grounds to hate it. For
with the Queensberrys, he had, in effect, found the place in
the great world he had been searching for. The world of
Amesbury and Middleton Stoney and the house in Burlington Gardens was a wholly acceptable substitute for St. James's
and Richmond and Whitehall; the Duchess, as Gay himself
had written earlier, was 'in Place of a Queen' to him; he
enjoyed the confidence and trust of the Duke and served him
as he might have hoped to serve royalty, travelling with him
and helping him in his business affairs. 'I am not thinking of
a Court or performent,' he told Swift (4 July 1730 (No. 62)),
'for I think the Lady I live with is my friend, so that I am at
the height of my ambition.' Gay was court favourite here and,
moreover, a favourite who need never fear for his place. The
Queensberrys had already committed themselves to him in
a most extravagant and telling manner, and Gay, whose
capacity for belief and trust was limitless, responded in kind.

Thus the story has a happy ending, as is evident in the
tone of the letters of 1730–2. The relaxed atmosphere, the
mutual affection and trust of the Queensberry circle, per-
meate the joint letters from Gay and the Duchess to Swift
and to Mrs. Howard. Again and again the word 'happy'
appears; they envy no one; they have left off 'great folks'
and are sufficient unto themselves. It is an idyllic existence:
'Were I to live here never so long I believe I should never
think of London', Gay informed Swift from Amesbury,
8 November 1730 (No. 65). He was occasionally called
upon to assist the Duke, but generally he had little to do but
write (when he was in the mood), enjoy his independence,
husband his modest fortune and, above all, indulge his pen-
chant for trivia and whimsy. The letters of these later years
are crowded with small talk and *jeux d'esprit*. Gay teases the
Duchess about her painting and her needlework, and the
Duke about the hunt getting out of hand and overrunning
the chicken yard; he protests that the Duchess is so niggardly
that she will not let him buy a new pair of shoes; there is the
problem of whether white currants are proper for making
tarts, and talk of Stephen Duck, and the running joke

concerning Swift's preposterous 'articles', which must be agreed to before he will visit Amesbury.

In all, the world had at last fulfilled the promises it had held out and Gay was able to announce to Swift from Amesbury on 4 July 1730 (No. 62) that he was now resolved to 'pass away Life as agreeably as I can in the way I am'—which is perhaps all he ever really wanted to do.

THE PRESENT EDITION

The texts of the letters are reproduced *literatim*, with the following exceptions:

1. All raised letters (M^r, D^r, ł, etc.) have been lowered;
2. the old-style 'y' for 'th' has been modernized, and abbreviations beginning with the 'y' form have been expanded, i.e. 'y^t' is printed as 'that';
3. common abbreviations, such as S^r, wth, w^{ch}, y^r, Servt, have been expanded;
4. in a few instances where punctuation may reasonably be assumed to have existed, but is no longer legible in the manuscript, it has been supplied; and these, as well as all other emendations, are indicated by brackets.

The heading of each letter provides the following information: writer(s) and addressee(s), date and provenance.

In the case of letters for which dates have been assigned by the editor or by others, this fact is indicated by placing the dates in brackets. The basis for the dating is explained in a footnote.

The provenances of Gay's letters are of two sorts: manuscripts (Gay autographs or transcripts, usually contemporary) and printed versions. If the text has been taken from a manuscript, the current location of the manuscript is given. Manuscripts now in the British Museum are identified by the addition number. Transcripts have been identified as such in the footnotes; all other manuscripts may be presumed to be autographs. If the text has come from a printed source, the date of first publication and an abbreviated title of the source is given. A list of these abbreviated titles will be found below.

The reader will recognize the similarity of this arrangement to that adopted by Professor Sherburn in *The Correspondence of Alexander Pope*.

A brief word about the footnotes. In general, the design of the footnotes is to provide the information or clarification which the reader might reasonably expect, in the most economical manner possible. Despite this effort toward economy, some of the footnotes have turned out to be lengthy, because of the necessity to summarize previous scholarship or to document in detail. In these instances it was felt that it would be better to err on the side of thoroughness. At the same time the editor has tried to avoid being jejune and annotating the text away. Out of respect for the reader's intelligence, many figures who appear prominently in the letters—Charles Jervas, William Pulteney, John Arbuthnot, Thomas Parnell, to mention a few—have not been further identified. Some readers may, perhaps, feel that more information might have been supplied, and some, no doubt, will be convinced that there is here already the little more than a little which is by much too much. In sum, every editor is confronted with a variant of Hamlet's dilemma which might be expressed as 'to annotate or not to annotate'. In every instance of making this arbitrary decision, the editor pleads good faith and the best of intentions.

Lexington, Virginia

ABBREVIATIONS

DNB = *Dictionary of National Biography*, 63 vols., 1885–1900.
Earls = James Lees-Milne, *Earls of Creation*, 1962.
Early Career = George Sherburn, *The Early Career of Alexander Pope*, 1934.
Favorite = William H. Irving, *John Gay, Favorite of the Wits*, 1940.
GEC = George E. Cokayne, *et al.*, *The Complete Peerage*, 13 vols., 1910–59.
Journal = Jonathan Swift, *Journal to Stella*, ed. Harold Williams, 2 vols., 1948.
Letters of Mr. Alexander Pope = *Letters of Mr. Alexander Pope, and Several of his Friends*, 1737.
Letters of Pope = *Letters of Mr. Pope, and Several Eminent Persons, From the Year 1705, to 1711*, 1735.
Letters to Ford = *Letters from Jonathan Swift to Charles Ford*, ed. D. Nichol Smith, 1935.
Life of Parnell = Oliver Goldsmith, 'Life of Parnell', prefixed to *Poems on Several Occasions*, 1770.
Minor Poems = Alexander Pope, *Minor Poems*, ed. Norman Ault and John Butt (vol. vi of the Twickenham Edition), 1954.
NED = *A New English Dictionary on Historical Principles*, 10 vols., 1888–1928.
New Light = Norman Ault, *New Light on Pope*, 1949.
Original Letters = *Original Letters from Richard Baxter, et al.*, ed. Rebecca Warner, 1817.
Poetical Works = *The Poetical Works of John Gay*, ed. G. C. Faber, 1926.
Pope Corr. = *The Correspondence of Alexander Pope*, ed. George Sherburn, 5 vols., 1956.
Posthumous Letters = *Posthumous Letters from Various Celebrated Men Addressed to Francis Colman and George Colman, the Elder*, ed. George Colman, the Younger, 1820.
Spence, *Anecdotes* = Joseph Spence, *Anecdotes, Observations, and Characters, of Books and Men*, 1820.
Suffolk Corr. = *Suffolk Correspondence*, ed. John W. Croker, 2 vols., 1824.

Swift Corr. = *The Correspondence of Jonathan Swift*, ed. Harold Williams, 5 vols., 1963–5.

Thomas Tickell = R. E. Tickell, *Thomas Tickell and the Eighteenth Century Poets, 1685–1740*, 1931.

ACKNOWLEDGEMENTS

The following institutions have furnished photostatic or microfilm reproductions of manuscript letters: The Bodleian Library, The British Museum, Harvard University (The Houghton Library), The Historical Society of Pennsylvania, The Huntington Library, The Pierpont Morgan Library, Trinity College Library (Dublin), Yale University Library.

Reproductions or transcripts of manuscript letters have been furnished by individuals as follows: The Marquess of Bath, Lord Congleton, T. Cottrell-Dormer, Mr. and Mrs. Donald F. Hyde, The Duke of Portland, Lord Rothschild, Robert H. Taylor.

The editor is further obliged to these institutions and these individuals for their kindness in granting publication permission.

Other transcripts were made from the following printed sources: Ayre, *Memoirs of Pope* (1745), *Letters of Mr. Alexander Pope* (1737), *Letters of Pope* (1735), *Letters of Pope and Swift* (1740), 'Life of Parnell' (1770), *Original Letters* (1817), *Posthumous Letters* (1820), *Thomas Tickell* (1931).

Many people have helped in many ways in the preparation of this volume and some of these deserve better than generalized recognition. They are: Robert J. Barry, Jr., David Baxandall, Charles E. Beckwith, Esmond S. de Beer, Dorothy W. Bridgwater, The Duke of Buccleuch, Herbert Cahoon, Frank G. G. Carr, John Carswell, C. E. R. Clarabut, James L. Clifford, W. D. Coates, Herbert Davis, Vinton Dearing, Charles P. Finlayson, J. D. Fleeman, David F. Foxon, E. Gaskell, Martin G. Hamlyn, Geoffrey Handley-Taylor, Paul D. A. Harvey, R. H. Ingleton, William H. Irving, William Kellaway, R. W. Ketton-Cremer, James Lees-Milne, W. R. Le Fanu, The Marquess of Londonderry, J. C. Maxwell, Rex Morgan, Richard T. Morris, A. N. L. Munby, Francis Needham, James M. Osborn, William O'Sullivan, T. S. Pattie, W. W. Percival-Prescott, Ricardo Quintana, C. J. Rawson, James S. Ritchie, T. V. Roberts, Sybil Rosenfeld, W. R. Savadge, William E. Schultz, Robert Shackleton, the late George Sherburn, F. Taylor, G. Turner, R. P. F. White, Reginald Williams, S. W. Woodward, Thomas S. Wragg, and the Staff of the Preston Library, Virginia Military Institute. The editor's son, C. F. Burgess III, devoted many hours to the vexing but vital chore of proof-reading.

Finally, the generous support of the American Philosophical Society (Penrose Fund) and the V.M.I. Foundation is especially acknowledged.

1. Gay *to* Nicholas Dennis[1] *10 January 1705*

Robert H. Taylor Collection (Princeton, N.J.)

Londo: Janr: 10: 1705

Coz: Dennis[2] / I sent your bed away last Thursday sevenight the Carriage paid to Exon, directed to Mr Atheys [Atkeys?] as you orderd, the bed comes to łı6, and with it I sent you an easy chair of the same as the bed, which my Mistress advisd me, being very usefull, & fashionable he hath made the best sort, it comes to ł3, I hope they will please you, I am at present much out of order,[3] I have not heard as yet what the frames that the bed, & chair is put up in, comes to, but I will not fail of giving an account of every thing in a post or two, I have sent you herein the carriers note for the carriage, pray tell Coz: Richd Parmynter,[4] that Mr Rolles hath paid me for his neckcloths. my service to all freinds. I am your Loving freind / & Humble Servant / John Gay.

Address: To Mr Nicho Dennys Merchant / In Barnstaple Devon
Postmark: IA/10
Endorsement: Letter of Gay the / Poet Written when / he was with the silk / mercer 1705 [Unknown hand]

[1] This is the earliest Gay letter known to be extant.

[2] Nicholas Dennis (1679–1760), merchant, householder, and subscriber to the laying out of the Square in Barnstaple in 1715. The appellation 'Cousin' is probably meaningless since Gay was at best a distant kinsman of Dennis through their mutual connexion with the Fortescue family. I am indebted to Mr. Alfred E. Blackwell, Librarian of the North Devon Athenaeum, for this information.

[3] Gay was unhappy with his lot as a draper's clerk and was released from his indenture in the summer of 1706. See *Favorite*, p. 27.

[4] Again, 'Cousin' is evidently honorific. Nicholas Dennis's mother, Jane, was a Parminter but there is no evidence of a direct tie between the Gay and Parminter families.

2. Gay *to* Maurice Johnson, Jr.[1] *13 January 1713*

Harvard University

Sir / I could not but lay hold on this occasion of returning you my thanks for all your former favours; and I must confess, I have deferr'd it longer than otherwise I should have done to wait for this oppertunity. I cannot as yet give you any Account of the success of the Poem,[2] this being the first Day of it's being Published. Her Grace & Lady Isabella[3] seem not displeased with my offering: I hope when you criticize, you will remember I am your Friend. but I need not put you in mind of that, since you have already given such sincere proofs of your Friendship towards / Your most obliged Humble / Servant / John Gay.

London. / Janr. 13. 1713.

Pray present my humble / service to your father.

Address: To / Maurice Johnson junr Esqr / at Spalding in / Lincoln-shire.
Postmark: IA/13
Endorsement: From Mr Gay / with Rural Sports a Poem [Johnson's hand]
Frank: W: Livingston:

3. Gay *to* Maurice Johnson, Jr. *23 April 1713*

Harvard University

Sir / I had not neglected writing you a line or two of the Town News when I sent you Mr Pope's Poem, had I not been at that time in Company, & I was loath to deferr your Entertainment in Windsor Forrest a Post longer. Cato affords universal discourse, & is received with great

[1] Attorney, antiquary, and founder of 'The Gentlemen's Society' at Spalding, of which Gay was probably an honorary member. See *DNB* entry for 'Johnson'. Through Johnson, Gay was introduced into the household of the Duchess of Monmouth, where he served as domestic steward from 1712 to 1714.

[2] *Rural Sports*, which was dedicated to Pope.

[3] Lady Isabella Scott, daughter of the Duchess of Monmouth.

applause. my Lord Oxford, Lord Chancellor and the Speaker
of the House of Commons have bespoke the Box on the Stage
for next Saturday: the Character of Cato is a man of strict
Vertue, & a Lover of his Country; the Audience for several
Nights clapp'd some Particular parts of the Play which they
thought reflected upon the Tories; some passages in the
Prologue were strained that way too; viz. this Passage

> These tears shall flow from a more gen'rous Cause
> Such tears as Patriots shed for dying Laws,

never faild of raising a loud Clap; but you see that the
Ministry are so far from thinking it touches them, that the
Treasurer and Chancellor will honour the Play with their
Presence. here hath been a Poem lately published called Peace,
which, 'tis said Trapp[1] was the Author of; there are a great
many good lines in the Poem, & he hath here and there mixed
some reflections on the late Ministry. my Play[2] comes on, on
the 5th of May; it was put off upon account of Cato; so that you
may easily imagine I by this time begin to be a little sensible
of the approaching Danger. pray present my humble service
to your father; and believe me, when I tell you that I am /
Your most obliged Humble Servant / J Gay.

April. 23. 1713.

Address: For Maurice Johnson junr Esqr / at Spalding in / Lincolnshire
Postmark: AV/23 [Indistinct]
Endorsement: Mr Gay Play of Cato / Peace Trapps Poem / Aprill
1713 [Johnson's hand]

4. Gay *to* William Fortescue[3] *5 October* [*1713*]

The Pierpont Morgan Library

Dear Sir / You must know that I yesterday made an
attempt to repay you with a Letter in French, & having no

---

[1] Joseph Trapp (1679–1747), poet
and pamphleteer. Trapp committed
the same political blunder as did Gay
in *The Shepherd's Week* in dedicating
'Peace, a Poem' to the ill-fated Bolingbroke. Swift called Trapp's effort 'a
dull Poem'. See *Journal*, ii. 650.

[2] *The Wife of Bath*, produced 12 May
1713 at Drury Lane. Gay's misgivings
about his play were well founded. It ran
three nights to indifferent audiences.

[3] The year is arrived at through Gay's

Dictionary & being but a poor Proficient in that Polite tongue, I was forced to give over this grand undertaking.[1] I had begun to acquaint you that I was last Week a Shooting with my Lord Essex[2] who leaves England next Week in order to make the Tour of Italy & France; and when I came to the word Shooting; I was forced to express myself in a Poetical Manner by having recourse to Boileau, & call it

Faire le Guerre aux habitans de l'air

and when I would have told you that we owed our Game to Dogs called Pointers, I was obliged in a tedious Circumlocution to tell you, that we had Dogs that lying themselves down, would direct us to the Birds. and when I would have acquainted you with our Success, I could not find a word for Poachers after a half an hours Study. besides, if I had proceeded, I consider'd I should have wholy neglected Sentiments, and only just filled up a Paper with French Phrases that I could have at the time recollected; for if I was to accost a French Man, I should certainly begin with that impertinent Compliment, Monsieur Comment vous portez vous? and a hundred to one if we were consulting a Sundial, to show my Learning I should add Quelle heure est il? and should haul into our Discourse some other as insignificant Questions which I had just learnt in my Grammar. I hope these reasons will satisfy you for my not writing in an unknown tongue. Here's a Melancholy prospect before my Eyes; I am now looking upon the Grove, which is now every day losing its Shade; and alas! what it is [*sic*] a Grove without a Shade; the leaves fall; the Bowling Green is Wet, the Roads are Dirty and I almost wish to be in London, where Pope hath been all this Summer, & Budgell is still of the same opinion when I last saw him which is about a Month since that all the Ladies are Rascals. I have just finish'd a Poem which I wrote since I came to Moore Parke,[3] as I sent

---

reference to his poem, *The Fan*, published on 8 December 1713, as 'just finish'd'.

[1] Gay was an indifferent linguist and, perhaps, something of a Francophobe. See Letter 24; see also his *Epistle to the Right Honourable William Pulteney, Esq.* (1720).

[2] William Capell (1697–1743), 3rd Earl of Essex. Gay's acquaintance with the Earl was later enlarged by Essex's marriage to Jane Hyde, sister of Gay's friend and champion, Catherine, Duchess of Queensberry.

[3] The Duchess of Monmouth's estate in Hertfordshire.

you a Specimen of the Rural Sports, I here send you a
Sample of this new Production. The Poem is upon a Fan,
wherein I have in some measure followed Virgils & Homer's
Shield, in the Description of its painting & Invention; I
have introduced Gods & Goddesses & others of little
inferior Dignity. tis in lenghth about 700 lines, but in
Goodness I am afraid not above 100. when you see it I don't
question but you will give me your impartial opinion, till
then take this; tis part of a Digression about Dress.

> What thought what pompous Numbers can express
> Th' inconstant Equipage of female Dress?
> How the strait Stays the Slender Waste constrain,
> Or How t'adjust the Mantoe's sweeping train?
> What Fancy can the Petticoat Surround
> With the capacious hoop of Whalebone bound?
> But stay, presumptuous Muse, nor Boldly dare,
> The Toilette's sacred Mysteries Declare;
> Let a just distance be to Beauty paid,
> None Here must Enter but the trusty Maid.
> Should you the Wardrobe's Magazine Rehearse,
> And glossy Mantoes rustle in thy Verse,
> Should you the rich Brocaded Suit unfold
> Where rising flow'rs grow stiff with frosted Gold,
> The dazled Muse Would from her subject stray,
> And in a Maze of Fashions lose her Way.[1]

Adieu / Dear Mr Fortescue. / J Gay
Octr. 5.

Term begins the latter end / of this Month.

Address: For William Fortescue Esqr. / at Fallowpit near Kings-
bridge. / in / Devon
Postmark: 7/o[c?]

5. Gay *to* Addison[2] [*December 1713*]

1931 (*Thomas Tickell*)

Sir / I have sent you only two Copys of my Poems though

---

[1] *The Fan*, i. 229–44. Prior to publication, Gay made some revisions in this
passage.

[2] This letter was first printed by R. E.
Tickell in *Thomas Tickell and the
Eighteenth Century Poets, 1685–1740*

by your Subscription you are entitled to ten, whatever Books you want more Tonson or Lintot upon your sending will deliver.

I cannot neglect this Occasion of returning you my thanks for the Benefits you have done me & I beg you to believe that I have such a just sense of them, if you even could think of doing more for me, you could not ingage me further to you, for tis impossible to owe you more Love & Gratitude than I do already / I am Sir &c / JOHN GAY

6. Gay *to* Parnell[1] [*April–May 1714*]

Congleton MSS.

> Ye Chariots rolling through the Street
> Ye Operas with voices Sweet
> Ye Ladies dress'd in rich array
> That walk the Park or grace the Play
> Ye Balls, Assemblees Tea & Ombre
> And other Pleasures without *Nombre*

(1931), p. 77, from a copy found in Tickell's letter book, and is reprinted here by permission of the publisher, Constable & Co., Ltd.

My dating is based on Gay's reference to the subscription copies due to Addison. Irving believes that *Trivia*, published 26 January 1716 by Lintot, is the poem in question and, accordingly, dates the letter January 1716. See *Favorite*, p. 126; Sherburn concurs in this dating, see *Early Career*, p. 155, n. 1. However, in view of Gay's devastating burlesque of Addison's *Cato* in *The What D'ye Call It*, less than a year earlier, it is difficult to conceive of Addison, never a magnanimous man, subscribing for ten copies of a work of Gay's. On the other hand, until the attack in *The What D'ye Call It* appeared, Addison had every reason to feel kindly toward Gay. In *The Present State of Wit* (1711) Gay singled out *The Spectator* as the best of the London journals, and in his *Epistle to Bernard Lintott* (1712) he made Addison the peer of Ovid and Homer. See also Pope to Addison, 30 July 1713, *Pope Corr*. i. 184, wherein Pope describes Gay as a zealous friend and 'honourer' of Addison. Thus, I would date the letter prior to *The What D'ye Call It* and before the Pope–Addison rift. *The Fan*, a poem in three books published by Tonson on 8 December 1713, when harmony still prevailed among the Wits, qualifies equally well as 'my Poems'. I have searched in vain for subscription lists of both poems which would, of course, resolve the matter.

[1] Dated from various internal evidence by C. J. Rawson who first printed this letter in *Review of English Studies*, N.S. x (1959), 373–4. Although the manuscript is a copy, the letter is undoubtedly genuine. See Rawson, p. 371; see also Letter 20, n. 1.

Oh Dear Doctor Parnelle, whats all your Trees, your Meadows, your Streams & Plains to a walk in St James's Park, I hope you wont be so profane as to make any comparison of the sight of a Cow & a Calf to a Beau & a Belle? do you imagine a Place beneath a shady Back[1] of equal value, to a Place at Court? no, no, good Doctor, our good & pious Friend Pope stands now at your Elbow ready to confute all these praises of the Country,[2] he knows you can speak as well in the praise of great Men as of great Trees, & that you would as soon go to a Minister of States Levee, as look on a Haycock, or walk in a Dale. Mr Pope knows I dont care for the trouble of writing, I mean transcribing, & therefore you must not take a blot now & then for want of due respect, besides, I have still the excuse of a sore throat, & a Hoarse, Mr Barnevelt[3] was here, this evening, & entered into a learned Conferrence with me concerning Homer, he tells me he very much suspects, the accounts we have of that Poet & doubts whether there were ever such a Person in being; he made the same Remark upon Virgil, & Horace & the rest of the Poetical tribe, so that Hardoine[4] hath now found a person to fall in with his oppinions, he complains of Dr Clarke's Book of the Trinity,[5] very much laments the corruption of Politicks, & bewails the absence of Mr Pope. The Dean & I met as usual at Dr Arbuthnot's & the Earle was angry that we did not make him the usual Compliment,[6] Martin still is under the Doctor's hands, & flourishes, I will be sure to take care of those things you mention, / I am, / yours most Sincerely
you have no Letters

[1] 'Bank' would provide a better reading here, but the manuscript is clearly 'Back'.

[2] Parnell and Pope were then at Binfield working on the translation of the *Iliad*.

[3] Evidently an actual person, to begin with, whose name the Scriblerians appropriated, or to whom they gave the fictitious name, 'Esdras Barnivelt'. Ultimately, he assumed mythical proportions, much like Scriblerus, and epitomized the pedant. Pope used the name as a pseudonym for *A Key to the Lock* (1715).

[4] Jean Hardouin (1646–1729), a French scholar who maintained that many of the classics had actually been written in the thirteenth century.

[5] *The Scripture Doctrine of the Trinity* (1712) by Samuel Clarke.

[6] Gay's meaning is somewhat obscure. Oxford evidently complained either because he was not invited to the Scriblerians' meeting, or because he was not subjected to their raillery, the 'Compliment' usually accorded him.

7. Gay *to* Swift[1] *8 June* [*1714*]

Add. 4804

London June. 8th.

Sir / Since you went out of Town My Lord Clarendon
was appointed Envoy Extraordinary to Hanover in the room
of Lord Paget, and by making use of those Friends which I
entirely [ow]e to you, He hath accepted me for his Secretary.[2] this day by [ap]pointment I met his Lordship at Mr
Secretary Bromley's office, [MS. torn] he then order'd me to
be ready by Saturday. I am quite off [from] the Dutchess of
Monmouth. Mr Lewis was very ready to serve [me] upon
this occasion, as was Dr Arbuthnot & Mr Ford.[3] I am every
day attending my Lord Treasurer for his Bounty in order to
set me out, which he hath promised me upon the following
Petition which I sent him by Dr Arbuthnot.

> The Epigrammatical Petition of John Gay.
> I'm no more to converse with the Swains
> But go where fine People resort
> One can live without Money on Plains,
> But never without it at Court,
>
> If when with the Swains I did Gambol
> I arrayd me in silver and blue[4]
> When abroad & in Courts I shall ramble
> Pray, My Lord, how much Money will do?

We had the Honour of the Treasurer's Company last
Saturday when we sate [sat] upon Scriblerus; Pope is in
Town, & hath brought with him the first Book of Homer.
I am this evening, to be at Mr Lewis's with the Provost Mr

[1] Gay's appointment as Secretary to
Clarendon establishes the year as 1714.

[2] Edward Hyde (1661–1724), 3rd
Earl of Clarendon. A desperate Tory
gamble to win influence at Hanover, the
Clarendon Mission's chances of success
were doubtful at best, and with the
death of Queen Anne on 1 August the
failure of the undertaking was ensured.
For Gay the venture into diplomacy
proved disastrous. He had given up his
sinecure with the Duchess of Monmouth
in order to join Clarendon and he returned to London in the autumn of 1714
without immediate plans or prospects.

[3] Charles Ford (1682–1743?), of
Woodpark, co. Meath, lifelong friend
and sometime companion of Swift. He
was then serving as Gazetteer.

[4] See also the Prologue to *The Shepherd's Week*, l. 40.

Ford Parnell & Pope. 'tis thought my Lord Clarendon will make but a short stay at Hannover.[1] if 'twas possible, that any recommendation could be procur'd, to make me more distinguish'd than ordinary during my Stay at that Court I should think myself very happy if you could contrive any Method to procure it; for I am told that their Civilitys very rarely descend so low as the Secretary. I have all the reason in the World to acknowledge this as wholy owing to you, and the many favours I have receiv'd from you purely out of your Love for doing Good assures me you will not forget me in my absence; as for myself whether I am at home or abroad, Gratitude will always put me in mind of the Man to whom I owe so many Benefits / I am / Your most obliged / Humble Servant / J Gay.

Address: For the Reverend Dr Swift Dean / of St Patricks
Endorsement: Gay / Jun. 8. 1714 [Swift's hand]

8. Gay *to* Robert Harley, Earl of Oxford
10 June 1714

Portland MSS. (B.M. Loan 29/203)

Thursday June. 10. 1714.

My Lord / Your Lordships continued Goodness towards me makes me presume to remind your Lordship of your Shepherd's Petition.[2] my Lord Clarendon tells me, he sends his things down the Water to morrow and embarks on Saturday. the Time to provide myself is very short; but I submit myself entirely to your Lordships Will and Pleasure, and now attend your Lordships Commands. / My Lord / Your Lordships / most dutifull, / most obedient / Humble Servant / John Gay.

---

[1] Actually three months. Gay left London for the Continent on 14 June and was back in town by mid September. See Pope to Gay, 23 September 1714, *Pope Corr.* i. 254.

[2] See Letter 7.

9. Gay *to* Charles Ford[1] *27 June* [*1714*]

The Historical Society of Pennsylvania

Sunday. June 27.

From aboard the Henrietta in Margett Road.

Sir / You may observe my head begins to turn by my beginning my Letter at wrong end of the Paper. I am just this Minute going to be sea sick, there being now a brisk Gale but directly against us. you can scarce imagine the happiness I have had since I came aboard; you can only toast the Lady that hath been aboard of us two days successively, my Lady Theodosia[2] left us but Yesterday, & saild up the Medway to Rochester. think with what wistfull Lookes I saw the Boat push off from our Vessell when Matrimony & the Company of her Husband[3] would not allow her to cast one pitying Look behind.[4] now I talk of casting, I must tell you, If I dont make an end I shall be forc'd to cast up (what the sailors call) my Accounts. / I am Sir / Your most obliged / Humble Servant / J Gay.

Pray present my Humble Service / to Mr Lewis Dr Arbuthnot, the Dean / the rest of our friends & Compotators. / but you are not acquainted, I think, with / Lady Isabella![5]

Address: For Charles Ford Esqr. / at his office at Whitehall / London
Postmark: 29/IV

[1] Hitherto known only from an extract in the catalogue of Christie's Sale, 4 June 1896, printed by D. Nichol Smith in his *Letters to Ford*, p. 221. The letter is printed here in its entirety, from the original in the archives of the Historical Society of Pennsylvania.

[2] Clarendon's daughter.

[3] Theodosia was still a newly-wed in 1714, having married John Bligh, the future Baron Clifton, the year before.

See GEC, iii. 311. This, perhaps, accounts for her alleged circumspection.

[4] Nichol Smith suggested (*Letters to Ford*, p. 221, n. 2) that this passage '. . . anticipates "cast one longing ling'ring look behind" in Gray's *Elegy*'. What Gay actually wrote, however, was 'one pitying Look' and not 'one lingering look' as the extract read.

[5] Lady Isabella Scott.

10. Gay *to* Charles Ford *6 July 1714*

The Pierpont Morgan Library

Sir / After eleven days being on board & putting backwards and forwards in the Channell, not without a day or two's seasickness I am now at the Hague, where we came on sunday Evening from Roterdam. we are here in the midst of Treatys & Negotiations, Plenipotentiarys Embassadors & Envoys, but I not having, as yet enter'd the list of Politicians am wholy taken up, with observing the Ladys. here are assemblys almost every Night, I fear I shall scarce have the oppertunity to be at one of them; my Lady Straffords[1] is Wednesdays & Fridays. I have seen several Ladys that are pretty enough while they are in Holland; but should they once appear in Kensington Gardens, they must resign all their pretensions to Beauty.

> Nos patriae fines et dulcia linquimus arva
> Nos patriam fugimus, tu Tityre lentus in umbrà[2]

Doctor Parnell would translate the words in Umbra, at Ombre, but for my part, I believe you know how to treat a Lady as well in a Shade as at a gaming table, and that you had rather stick to the vulgar construction. as for myself, who know nothing of play, I would be glad to take up with an Arbour. There are shades at Bingfield, Mrs Fermor is not very distant from thence; make a visit to Pope and Parnelle, and while they are making a Grecian Campaign, do you as AEneas did before you meet your Venus in a Wood, he knew her by her *Locks* and so may you—but as you are a man of Honour & Modesty—think not of Hairs less in sight or any Hairs but these.[3] I am just this Minute going to take the air with my Lord at the House in the Wood, where if no Nymph disturbs my Meditations I will think of you,

[1] Thomas Wentworth (1672–1739), 3rd Earl of Strafford, was then Ambassador at the Hague.
[2] Virgil, *Eclogues*, i. 3–4. These lines

were apparently favourites of Gay's. See also Letter 20.
[3] *The Rape of the Lock*, iv. 176.

and our Sundays conferences. / I am / Your most obliged / Humble Servant / J Gay

July. 6. os. 1714.

In a day or two we set forward / for Hanover.

Address: For Charles Ford Esqr at his Office / at Whitehall / London

11. Gay *to* Charles Ford 7 *August 1714*

The Rothschild Library (Trinity College, Cambridge)

Hanovre Aug. 7. 1714.

Sir / This comes to put you to a further trouble in relation to my Works; the Princess[1] hath now ask'd me for my Poem, and I am obliged to make Presents to three or four Ladys besides, so that I must desire you to send me three or four *Shepherd's Weeks* more with as Many Poem's of the Fan, if you send your Servant; Tonson will supply you with them. I go every night to Court at Herenhausen, the Place & Gardens more than answer'd my expectations. if it were not for the Princess and the Countess of Picbourg[2] I should forget my faculty of Speech, for I cannot as yet take the Courage to address a Lady in French and both those Ladys take a pleasure in speaking English, which I thank God, notwithstanding I have pass'd through the regions of Westphalia I have not quite forgot. the Court have a notion that I am to reside here upon his Lordship's return, and I have received many Compliments upon that occasion; my Denial of it they look upon as a Sketch of my Politicks. the Princess and the Countess of Picbourg have both subscrib'd to Pope's Homer, and her Highness did me the Honour to say, she did not doubt it would be well done, since I recommended it. I had a design of writing to the Dean, but my Lord Clarendon hath just this Minute sent me a Long Letter to Copy, so that I shall be able to write nothing to him this Post, and to add

[1] The future Queen Caroline.
[2] The Countess of Piquebourg, shortly to accompany the Princess to England as Lady-in-Waiting.

nothing further to you. but that I am / Your most obliged Humble / Servant. / JG.

Mr Lewis shall hear from me soon. / if the Books are not sent with Expedition / I shall lose my Credit.

12. Gay *to* Arbuthnot *or* Swift *16 August 1714*

Add. 4804

Dear Sir. / You remember, I suppose, that I was to write you abundance of Letters from Hanover; but as one of the most distinguishing Qualities of a Politician is secrecy, you must not expect from me any Arcanas of State; there is another thing that is necessary to establish the Character of a Politician, which is, to seem always to be full of Affairs of State, to know the Consultations of the Cabinet Council, when at the same time all his Politicks are collected from Newspapers. which of these two causes my secrecy is owing to, I leave you to determine. there is yet one thing more that is extreamly necessary for a foreign Minister, which he can no more be without than an Artisan without his Tools, I mean the Terms of his Art, I call it an Art or a Science, because I think the King of France hath establish'd an Academy to instruct the young Machivillians of his Country in the deep and profound Science of Politicks. to the end that I might be qualified for an Employment of this Nature, and not only be qualified myself, but (to speak in the stile of Sir John Falstaff) be the cause of Qualification in others; I have made it my business to read Memoires, Treatys, &c. and as a Dictionary of Law terms is thought necessary for young Beginners so I thought a Dictionary of terms of state would be no less usefull for young Politicians. the Terms of Politicks being not so numerous as to swell into a Volume especially in time of Peace, for In time of War all the terms of Fortification are included; I thought fit to extract them in the same Manner for the benefit of young Practitioners, as a famous Author hath compiled his Learned Treatise of the

Law called the Doctor and Student.[1] I have not made any great Progress in this Peice, but however, I will just give you a Specimen of it, which will make you in some manner a judge of the Design, and Nature of this Treatise.

Politician. / What are the Necessary Tools for a Prince to work with?

Student. / Ministers of State.

Politician. / What are the two great Qualities of a Minister of State?

Student. / Secrecy, and Dispatch.

Politician. / Into how many parts are the Ministers of State divided?

Student. / Into two. first Ministers of State at home. secondly. Ministers of State abroad, who are called foreign Ministers.

Politician. / very right. now as I design you for the latter of these Employments, I shall wave saying any thing of the first of these. what are the different Degrees of foreign Ministers?

Student. / The different degrees of foreign Ministers are as follows first Plenipotentiarys, second Embassadors Extraordinary, third, Embassadors in Ordinary, fourth, Envoys Extraordinary, fifth Envoys in Ordinary, sixth, Residents, seventh. Consuls, and Eighth Secretarys.

Politician. / How is a Foreign Minister to be known?

Student / By his Credentials.

Politician. / When are a foreign Ministers Credentials to be delivered?

Student. / Upon his first admission into the Presence of the Prince to whom he is sent, otherwise called his first Audience.

Politician. / How many kinds of Audiences are there.

Student / Two, which are called a Publick Audience and a Private Audience.

Politician. / What should a Foreign Minister's Behaviour be when he has his first Audience?

Student / He should bow profoundly, speak deliberately, and wear both sides of his long Perriwig before. / &c.

---

[1] By Christopher Saint German. It was first published in the sixteenth century and became, like Blackstone's *Commentaries*, a standard law text.

by these few Questions and Answers you may be able to make some judgment of the usefullness of this Politick Treatise. Wiquefort tis true, can never sufficiently be admired for his Elaborate Treatise of the Conduct of an Embassador in all his Negotiations.[1] but I design this only as a Compendium, or the Embassador's Manual, or Vade Mecum. I have wrote so far of this Letter, and do not know who to send it to. but I have now determined to send it either to Doctor Arbuthnot or the Dean of St Patricks, or to both. my Lord Clarendon is very much approved of at Court, and I believe is not dissatisfied with his Reception. We have not much variety of Diversions, what we did yesterday & to day we shall do to morrow, which is, go to Court and walk in the Gardens at Heernhausen. if I write any more, my Letter will be just like my Diversions, the same thing over and over again, so / Sirs / Your most obliged Humble / Servant J Gay.

Hanover / Aug. 16. 1714.

I would have writ this Letter over again / but I had not time, [to] correct all Errata's.

Address: For Dr Arbuthnot or the / Dean of St Patricks.
Endorsement: Gay. / Hannovr Aug. 15th / 1714 [Swift's hand]

13. Gay *to* Charles Ford *30 December 1714*

The Hyde Collection (Somerville, N.J.)

Sir

       Not that I'll wander from my native home,
       And tempting Dangers foreign Citys roam.
       Let Paris be the Theme of Gallia's Muse,
       Where Slav'ry treads the Streets in wooden shoes;
       Nor will I sing of Belgia's frozen Clime,
       And teach the clumsy Boor to skate in Rhime;
       Where, if the warmer Clouds in Rain descend
       No miry Ways industrous Steps offend,
       The rushing Flood from sloping Pavements pours
       And blackens the Canals with dirty show'rs.

---

[1] *The Ambassador and his Functions* (1681) by Abraham de Wicquefort.

Let others Naples' smoother Streets rehearse
Or with proud Roman Structures grace their Verse,
Where frequent Murders wake the Night with Groans,
And Blood in purple Torrents dyes the Stones.
Nor shall the Muse through narrow Venice stray,
Where Gondolas their painted Oars display.
Oh happy Streets, to rumbling Wheels unknown,
No Carts or Coaches shake the floating Town
Thus was of old Britannia's City blest
E'er Pride and Luxury her Sons possest;
Coaches and Chariots yet unfashion'd lay
Nor late invented Chairs perplex'd the Way.[1] &c

That &c signifies near 300 Lines. so much for Poetry; you may easily imagine by this progress, that I have not been interrupted by any Place at Court. Mr Domville[2] told me how to direct to you a day or two since as I accidentally met him in the Park. I have not heard any thing of Parnell or the Dean since you left England;[3] Pope has been in the Country near a [Month], but I expect him in Town this Week to forward the Printing his Homer, which is already begun to be printed off; he will publish his Temple of Fame as soon as he comes to Town;[4] Rowe hath finish'd his Play,[5] and Lintot told me just now, that he was made Clerk of the Council to the Prince. there was a Ball at Somerset House last Tuesday where I saw *the Dutchess*;[6] the Prince and Princess were there, and danc'd our English Country Dances. I have been studying these two or three Minutes for something [else] to write to you, but I find myself at a Loss, and can't say any thing but that I am / Sir / Your most obedient / Humble Servant / J Gay.

London / Decemr 30. 1714.

Address: To / Charles Ford Esqr to be left at / Sir Richard Chantillon's Banker / in / Paris

[1] *Trivia*, i. 83–104.
[2] William Domville, M.P. for co. Dublin, 1715–27, and friend of both Ford and Swift.
[3] With the collapse of the Tory Government, Ford was relieved of his post as Gazetteer and he retired to the Continent.
[4] Published 1 February 1715.
[5] *The Tragedy of Lady Jane Grey*, first acted 20 April 1715.
[6] Probably Gay's late patron, Anne Scott, Duchess of Monmouth, whom Gay would look upon as *the Duchess*.

14. Gay *to* Parnell[1] 29 *January* [*1714/15*]

Congleton MSS.

Dear Dr Parnell / 'Twas with a great deal of impatience, that I expected a Letter from you, for I concluded nothing but sickness cou'd hinder you from writing, to one, who loves you so well. I beg you, to take care of yourself, for I wou'd willingly, have you live as long as I do, & I have no great inclination to quit the world at present. your mouth shall soon, instead of receiving Physick pour forth Eloquence, & your arms, instead of being worn, to be let blood, shall distill Ink, upon paper from your Fingers-Ends to the immortalizing the great name of Zoilus.[2] now I am setting you at work perhaps you will ask how I'm employed myself. I have writ one book of the walking the streets, & among us we have just finish'd a Farce in Rhime, of one Act, which is now ready for the Stage.[3] 'tis upon the design I formerly have mention'd to you of a Country Gentleman's having a play acted by his Tenants. that you see something of the nature of it I have transcrib'd a speech of an Aunt to a Bench of Justices for saving her nephew from being Press'd.

> O Tyrant Justices, have you forgot
> how my poor Brother was in Flanders Shot?
> you press'd my Brother.—he shall walk in white
> He shall—and shake your Curtains eṽry Night
> what thoff a paultry Hare he rashly Kill'd
> That cross'd the Furrows while he plough'd the Field?
> you sent him o'er the Hills and far away
> left his old mother to the Parish pay
> with whome he shar'd his Ten Pence eṽry day
> *Wat* kill'd a Bird, was from his Farm turn'd out
> you took the law of *Thomas* for a Trout:

[1] The year is established by Gay's reference to his play, *The What D'ye Call It*, which was produced at Drury Lane on 23 February 1715. The Congleton manuscript is a copy, but see Letter 20, n. 1.

[2] Parnell's Life of Zoilus was prefixed to his translation of *Batrachomuomachia*, or *The Battle of the Frogs and the Mice*, thought at the time to be by Homer, published in May 1717.

[3] *The What D'ye Call It* is generally attributed to Gay but it is quite likely that Pope and Arbuthnot made some contributions. Gay, who was scrupulously honest in acknowledging literary indebtedness, thus says 'among us'.

you ruin'd my poor Uncle, at the Sizes
and made him pay *nine Pounds* for Nisiprizes.
now will you press my harmless Nephew too?
Ah! what has Conscience with the Rich to do
—Thoff in my Hand, no silver Tankard shine
nor my dry Lip is dy'd with Claret wine—
yet I can sleep in Peace—[1]

> The Justice / takes up a
> large / silver Tankard & /
> drinks

after this is play'd, I fully design, to pursue the Street Walking with Vigour, & let nothing interfere but a place, which at present, I have but little Prospects of, so that I must rub on[2] as well as I can in hope that Gazettes, will some time or other be my Friend. Rowe has finish'd his Play, and designs to go to the House with it this Week; Mr Pope is deeply engaged among Printers, & Booksellers; Phillips is made Paymaster to one of the Lotterys, and is publishing a Miscellany. all the Politicians are employ'd in Elections, and they search the News Papers for Whigs, & Torys just as I do the Lottery-Paper for my chance of one Tickett.[3] I see Mr Harcourt often & Dr Arbuthnot, & we never fail to remember you and the Dean, pray give my humble service to him, & forget not to write to me. / Dear Doctor Parnell I am / your most affectionate / Humble Servant / JG.

London / Janr. 29th.

15. Pope *and* Gay *to* Caryll[4] *3 March* [*1714/15*]

Add. 28618

March. 3d. 1714.

You travel like the sun, who, even while he retreats from us, darts back some rays of comfort. Your epistles in Mr

---

[1] *The What D'ye Call It*, I. i. 34–51.
[2] *NED* 'to contrive or make shift'.
[3] Gay perhaps means that the political managers were busy scanning newspaper accounts of marriages, deaths, appointments, etc., for hints of party sympathies. Or this may be a facetious reference to the 'parlor politicians'. I am indebted to Professor Benjamin Boyce for these suggestions.
[4] Add. 28618 is a copy.

Gay's behalf were sent, attended with a competence of tickets, to my Lord Waldegrave and Mr Plowden: the effect of 'em I do not yet know. You have obliged my friend and me beyond all power, and even decency of expression, and each of us ought to thank you for the other.

The farce has occasioned many different speculations in the town, some looked upon it as a mere jest upon the tragic poets, others as a satire upon the late war. Mr Cromwell[1] hearing none of the words and seeing the action to be tragical, was much astonished to find the audience laugh; and says the Prince and Princess must doubtless be under no less amazement on the same account. Several Templars and others of the more vociferous kind of critics, went with a resolution to hiss, and confessed they were forced to laugh so much that they forgot the design they came with. The Court in general has in a very particular manner come into the jest, and the first three nights (notwithstanding two of them were Court nights) were distinguished by very full audiences of the first quality. The common people of the pit and gallery received it at first with great gravity and sedateness, some few with tears; but after the third day they also took the hint, and have ever since been very loud in their clapps. There are still some grave sober men who cannot be of the general opinion, but the laughers are so much the majority, that Mr. Dennis and one or two more seem determined to undeceive the town at their proper cost, by writing some critical dissertations against it: to encourage them in which laudable design, it is resolved a preface shall be prefixt to the farce in the vindication of the nature and dignity of this new way of writing.

I have but just room to assure you of my most hearty service and lasting acknowledgments; for Mr Gay, who has wrought all the above said wonders, challenges a part of the paper. Believe me at all times / Dear sir / Your most affectionate faithful Friend / and Servant / A: P:

He will have made about an 100 ll. of this farce.

---

[1] Henry Cromwell, littérateur and man about town, who had introduced Gay to Pope. Cromwell was somewhat hard of hearing, which accounts for his mystification.

London March. 3. 1727.[1]

Sir / Now my Benefit Night is over, it should be my first care to return my thanks to those to whom I am mostly obliged; and the Civilitys that I have always received from you, and upon this occasion too claim this acknowledgment. The What dye call it met with more Success than could be expected from a thing so out of the way of the Common Taste of the Town. It has been play'd already five Nights, and the Gallerys who did not know what to make of it, now enter thoroughly into the humour, and it seems to please in general better than at first; the Parts in general were not so well play'd, as I could have wished, and in particular the Part of Filbert, to speak in the Style of the French Gazette Penketham did wonders; Mrs Bicknell perform'd miraculously, and there was much honour gained by Miss Younger tho' she was but a Parish Child. I hope next Week to have the honour to send you this dramatick Performance in Print, and I shall always think my self very happy when I can have any opportunity to shew myself / your most obliged Faithfull / humble Servant / J Gay.

16. Pope *and* Gay *to* Parnell[2] *18 March* [*1714/15*]

1770 (*Life of Parnell*)

London, March 18.

Dear Sir, / I must own I have long owed you a letter, but you must own, you have owed me one a good deal longer. Besides, I have but two people in the whole kingdom of Ireland to take care of; the Dean and you: but you have several who complain of your neglect in England. Mr. Gay complains, Mr. Harcourt complains, Mr. Jarvas complains, Dr. Arbuthnot complains, my Lord complains;[3] I complain. (Take notice of this figure of iteration, when you make your next sermon) some say, you are in deep discontent at the new

---

[1] The manuscript clearly reads '1727' but this is obviously an error.

[2] The year is inferred from the refer-

ences to the critical reception of *The What D'ye Call It.*

[3] Either Oxford or Bolingbroke.

turn of affairs; others, that you are so much in the Archbishop's good graces, that you will not correspond with any
that have seen the last ministry. Some affirm, you have
quarrel'd with Pope, (whose friends they observe daily fall
from him on account of his satyrical and comical disposition)
others, that you are insinuating yourself into the opinion of
the ingenious Mr. What-do-ye-call-him. Some think you are
preparing your sermons for the press, and others that you
will transform them into essays and moral discourses. But the
only excuse, that I will allow, is, your attention to the Life of
Zoilus, the Frogs already seem to croak for their transporta-
tion to England, and are sensible how much that Doctor is
cursed and hated, who introduced their species into your
nation; therefore, as you dread the wrath of St. Patrick, send
them hither, and rid your kingdom of those pernicious and
loquacious Animals.

I have at length received your poem out of Mr. Addison's
hands, which shall be sent as soon as you order it, and in what
manner you shall appoint. I shall in the mean time give
Mr. Tooke[1] a packet for you, consisting of divers merry
pieces. Mr. Gay's new Farce, Mr. Burnet's Letter to Mr.
Pope, Mr. Pope's Temple of Fame, Mr. Thomas Burnet's
Grumbler on Mr. Gay, and the Bishop of Ailsbury's Elegy,
written either by Mr. Cary or some other hand.

*Mr. Pope is reading a letter, and in the mean time, I make use
of the pen* to testify my uneasiness in not hearing from you.
I find success, even in the most trivial things, raises the indignation of scribblers: for I, for my What-d'-ye-call-it, could
neither escape the fury of Mr. Burnet, or the German
Doctor;[2] then where will rage end, when Homer is to be
translated? Let *Zoilus* hasten to your friend's assistance, and
envious criticism shall be no more. I am in hopes that we
may order our affairs so as to meet this summer at the Bath;
for Mr. Pope and myself have thoughts of taking a trip
thither. You shall preach, and we will write lampoons; for
it is esteemed as great an honour to leave the Bath, for fear

---

[1] Benjamin Tooke the Elder, formerly a Dublin printer and now bookseller
and financial agent in London for Swift
and others.

[2] *The What D'ye Call It* was attacked
by Thomas Burnet in *The Grumbler*,
17 March 1715, and by Philip Horneck
in his periodical, *The High-German Doctor*. See *Favorite*, pp. 112–13.

of a broken head, as for a Terrae Filius of Oxford[1] to be expelled. I have no place at court, therefore, that I may not entirely be without one every where, shew that I have a place in your remembrance; / Your most affectionate, / Faithful servant, / A. Pope, and J. Gay.

Homer will be published in three weeks.

17. Gay *and* Pope *to* Caryll[2] [*April 1715*]

Add. 28618

London.

Sir / Mr Pope is going to Mr Jervase's where Mr Addison is sitting for his Picture, in the mean time amidst Clouds of Tobaco at William's Coffee house I write this letter. we have agreed to spend this day in visitts; He is to introduce me to a Lord & two Ladys. and on my part which I think will ballance his Visitts, I am to present him to a Dutchess.[3] There is a grand Revolution at Wills' Coffee house; Morrice has quitted for a Coffeehouse in the Citty. and Titcomb[4] is restored to the great joy of Cromwell, who was at a great loss for a Person to converse with upon the Fathers' & Church History; the knowledge I gain from him is entirely in Painting & Poetry; & Mr Pope owes all his skill in Astro-

[1] A student orator and satirist. See 'Essay No. 1' in Nicholas Amhurst's *Terrae Filius: or, The Secret History of the University of Oxford* (1726).

[2] Dated from the references to *Jane Grey* (produced 20 April 1715) and Steele's knighthood (9 April 1715). Together with some additions from a joint letter to Caryll [19 March 1714/15], this letter became a letter from Pope and Gay to Congreve dated 7 April 1715. Neither of these letters is printed since Gay's contribution to the 19 March joint letter consists of a brief postscript and the 7 April letter to Congreve duplicates Gay's portion of the letter printed above. Add. 28618 is a copy. John C. Hodges argues that the 7 April letter to Congreve is a fabrication, a pastiche put

together by Pope when he came to edit his own correspondence in 1735 and found that the originals of his letters to Congreve had been lost. See *William Congreve: Letters and Documents* (1964), pp. 155–6.

[3] Probably the Duchess of Monmouth, Gay's former employer.

[4] Sherburn identified 'Titcomb' as Maj.-Gen. John Tidcombe. See *Pope Corr.* v. 222. This must be incorrect since Tidcombe died in 1713. See *DNB*; see also Charles Dalton, *English Army Lists and Commission Registers, 1661–1714* (1894), ii. 34, n. 6. Moreover, internal evidence leaves no room to question the dating of the letter. Gay also refers to a 'Titcomb' in *Mr. Pope's Welcome from Greece* (1720), l. 148.

nomy & particulary in the revolution of Eclipses to him and Mr Whiston, so celebrated of late for his discovery of the Longitude in an extraordinary Copy of verses which you hear'd when you were last in Town.[1] Mr Rowe's Jane Gray is to be play'd in Easter Week when Mrs Oldfield is to personate a Character directly opposite to female nature, for what Woman ever despised Soveraignty. Chaucer has a Tale, where a Knight saves his head by discovering that it was the thing which all Women most coveted; Colonel Frowde puns upon his Play, & declares that most of the Ladys of Drury Lane will not accept of a Crown when 'tis offerr'd them, unless you give them a supper into the Bargain; and wonders how people can admire the uncommonest of the Character. Mr Pope's Homer is retarded by the great Rains that have fallen of late, which causes the Sheetts to be long adrying, this gives Mr Lintott great uneasiness who is now endeavoring to corrupt the Curate of his Parish to pray for fair weather, that his Work may goe on the faster. There's a Sixpenny Criticism lately published upon the Tragedy of the What dye call it,[2] wherein he with much judgment & learning calls me a Blockhead, & Mr Pope a knave. his grand charge is agt the Pilgrims Progress being read, which he says is directly levell'd at Cato's reading Plato, to back this Censure, he goes on to tell you that the Pilgrims Progress being mention'd to be the eight Edition makes the Reflection Evident, the Tragedy of Cato being just eight times printed; He has allso endeavour'd to shew that every perticular Passage of the Play alludes to some fine part of [the] Tragedy which he says I've injudiciously & profanely abus'd. Sir Samuel Garth's Poem upon my Lord Clare's house I believe will be published in the Easter week.[3] My Lord Peterborough I hear is banished the Court, but I doe not know the occasion. Mr Pope and I have

---

[1] *A New Method for Discovering the Longitude both at Sea and Land* (1714). For a detailed account of this extraordinary document, see James M. Osborn, ' "That on Whiston" by John Gay', *Papers of the Bibliographical Society of America*, lvi (1962), 73–78.

[2] *A Compleat Key to the last New Farce The What D'ye Call It* (1715) is generally attributed to Lewis Theobald and Benjamin Griffin. For its role in the Pope–Addison controversy see *Early Career*, pp. 136–9.

[3] *Claremont*, a panegyric on the Earl of Clare's estate near Esher, Surrey, was published not in Easter Week, but on 2 May.

thoughts of doing ourselves the honour of making you a visitt in Sussex as soon as he hath ended this years Labour with the Bookseller, where I promise my self the greatest pleasure & satisfaction; may the Gout be favorable to you, that we may walk together in your Park; Mr Pope will make his Conditions before he will venture into your Company, that you shall not allow him any of your Conversation in the morning; he is oblig'd to pay this self denial in complaisance to his subscribers; for my part who doe not deall in Heroes or ravish'd Ladys, I may perhaps celebrate a milkmaid, describe the amours of your Parson's Daughter, or write an Elegy upon the death of a Hare; but my articles are quite the reverse of his, that you will interrupt me every morning, or ten to one I shall be first troublesome & interrupt you; let Mr Pope & Mr Homer keep company together, I should think that antient Gentleman a good Companion in a Garrett in London, but not in one of the pleasantest seats in England[1] where I hope next month to have the happiness of good Company.

Thus far Mr Gay—who in his letter has allready forestall'd all the subjects of Raillery & Diversion: unless it should be one, to tell you that I sitt up till one or two a Clock every night over Burgundy & Champaigne: and am become so much a modern Rake that I shall be ashamed in a short time to be thought to do any sort of business. I must get the Gout by drinking as above said, purely for a fashionable pretence to sitt still long enough to translate four books of Homer. I hope you'll by that time be up againe, and I may succeed to the Bed & Couch of my Predecessor at Ladyholt: Pray cause the stuffing to be repair'd, and the Crutches shorten'd for me. I have used my author like a mistress, attack'd at first with prodigious violence & warmth for a month or two, and then left him every day for any sort of idle Companion I cou'd light upon. It is with great grudging and malencholy that I now reflect I must at last be obliged to doe my drudgery at home, & stick to my old task & daily Labor.

That I may tell you some news of an other besides myself, know that Richard Steele Esqr is now Sir Richard Steele. what reflections may be made upon this occasion, I leave to

---

[1] Ladyholt, Caryll's estate in Sussex.

you to produce in your next Lucubration, which will be receiv'd with much pleasure by / Sir / your most affectionate faithfull / Friend & Servant / A. P.

18. Gay *to* Pope[1] *8 July 1715*

1735 (*Letters of Pope*)

July 8, 1715.

—I have just set down Sir *Samuel Garth* at the Opera. He bid me tell you, that every body is pleas'd with your Translation, but a few at *Button*'s; and that Sir *Richard Steele* told him, that Mr. *Addison* said *Tickel*'s translation was the best that ever was in any language. He treated me with extream civility, and out of kindness gave me a squeeze by the Sore finger.—I am inform'd that at *Button*'s your character is made very free with as to morals, &c. and Mr. *A*— says, that your translation and *Tickel*'s are both very well done, but that the latter has more of *Homer*. / I am, &c.

19. Gay, Jervas, Arbuthnot, *and* Pope *to* Parnell[2] [*February 1715/16*]

Trinity College, Dublin

My Dear Dr. / I was last Summer in Devonshire and am this Winter at Mrs Bouzer's[3] in the Summer I wrote a Poem & in the Winter I have publish'd it, which I have sent to you by Dr Elwood.[4] in the Summer I eat two dishes of Toadstools of my own gathering instead of Mushrooms, and in the Winter I have been sick with Wine as I am at this time,[5]

---

[1] This letter is known only from this excerpt first printed in the 1735 editions of *Letters of Mr. Pope, and Several Eminent Persons.*

[2] The dating is based on Gay's reference to *Trivia* (published 26 January 1716) as being already in print, and Arbuthnot's comment that volume ii of Pope's translation of the *Iliad* (published 22 March 1716) is forthcoming.

[3] Gay's landlady.

[4] Senior Fellow of Trinity College, Dublin, and one-time representative of the University in the Irish Parliament.

[5] The disjointed style of the letter testifies to Gay's fuzziness at the time of writing. Sherburn suggested that 'the writing is strongly redolent of wine' (*Pope Corr.* i. 331, n. 2).

[Two lines heavily scored out at this point][1] now you know where I have been and what I have done I shall tell you what I intend to do the ensuing Summer. I propose to do the same thing I did last, which was to meet you in any Part of England you would appoint, don't let me have two dissa-pointments. I have long'd to hear from you, and to that intent teaz'd you with three or four Letters, but having no Answers, I fear'd both your's & my Letters might have miscarried. I hope my Performance will please the Dean whom I often wish for, and whom I would have often wrote to, but for the same Reasons I neglected writing to you. I hope I need not tell you how I love you, & how glad I shall be to hear from you; which next to seeing you would be the greatest Satisfaction to / Your most Affectionate Friend & / Humble Servant JG.

Dear Mr A . . . n[2] / Tho' my Proportion of this Epistle shou'd be but a Sketch in Miniature yet I take up half this Page having paid my Club with the good Company both for our Dinner of Chops & for this Paper. The Poets will give you lively Descriptions in their Way, I shal only Acquaint you with that which is directly my own Province. I have just set the last hand to a Couplet,[3] for so I may call two Nymphs in One Piece—They are Pope's Favorites & therefore you will guess must have cost me more pains than any Nymphs can be worth. He has been so unreasonable to expect that I shoud have made them as beautifull upon Canvas as he has done upon paper. If this same Mr P . . . shou'd omit to write for the Dear Frogs & the Pervigilium I must entreat you not to let me languish for 'em as I have done ever since they crost the seas & us. You remember by what Neglects &c we mist 'em when we lost you & therefore I have not yet forgiven any of those Triflers that let 'em escape & run those

---

[1] Goldsmith printed this deletion in his Life of Parnell (1770) as: 'blessed be God for it, as I must bless God for all things. In the summer I spoke truth to damsels; in the winter I told lies to ladies.' The lines are illegible in a photocopy. The original can still be deciphered, however, and Mr. W. O'Sullivan, Keeper of Manuscripts at Trinity College, reports that Goldsmith's reading is substantially correct.

[2] 'Archdeacon'. Parnell was Arch-deacon of Clogher.

[3] Jervas's painting of Martha and Teresa Blount.

hazards. I am going on at the old rate & want you & the Dean prodigiously, and am in hopes of making you a Visit this Summer & of hearing from you both now you are together. Fortescue I am sure will be concern'd that he is not in Cornhill to set his ha[nd] to these presents not only as a Witness but as a Serviteur tres humble. C. Jerv[as].

It is so great an honour to a poor Scots man to be Rememberd at this time a day, especially by an inhabitant of the Glacialis Ierne that I take it very thankfully & have with my good freinds Rememberd you at our Table in the chop house in exchange Alley ther wanted nothing to compleat our happiness but Your Company & our dear Freind the Deans. I am sure the whole entertainment would have been to his Relish. Gay has gott so much money by his art of walking the streets, that he is ready to sett up his equipage. he is just going to the bank to negotiate some exchequer Bills. Mr pope delays his second volume of his Homer till the Martial Spirit of the Rebells is quite quelld it being judgd that his first part did some harm that way. Our love again & again to the Dear Dean. *fuimus Torys*: I can say no more—

When a man is conscious that he does no good himself, the next thing is to cause others to do some: I may claim some merit this way, in hastening this Testimonial from your Friends above-writing. Their Love to you indeed wants no Spur, their Ink wants no Pen, their Pen wants no Hand, their Hand wants no Heart, and so forth (after the manner of Rabelais, which is betwixt some meaning & no meaning.) And yet it may be said, when Present Thought and Opportunity is wanting, their Pens want Ink, their Hands want Pens, their Hearts want Hands, &c. Till Time, Place, and Conveniency concur, to sett them a writing; as at present, a sociable Meeting, a good Dinner, a warm Fire, and an easie Situation do, to the Joint Labour and pleasure of this Epistle.

Wherein, if I should say nothing, I should say much (much being included in my Love) tho my Love be such, that if I should say much, I should yet say nothing. it being (as Cowley says) equally impossible either to conceal, or to express it.

If I were to tell you the thing I wish above all things, it is to see you again; the next is to see here your Treatise of

Zoilus with the Batrachomuomachia, and the Pervigilium Veneris, both which Poems are Masterpieces in several kinds: and I question not the Prose is as excellent in its sort as the Essay on Homer:[1] Nothing can be more glorious to that great Author, than that the same hand that carvd his best Statue, and deckd it with its old Lawrells, should also hang up the Scare-crow of his miserable Critick, and gibbet up the Carcase of Zoilus to t[he T]error of the Witlings of Posterity.

More, much more, upon this & a thousand other s[ub]jects will be the matter of my next letter, whe[rein] I must open all the Friend to you. At this time I must be content with telling you I am faithfully / Your most affectionate & humble Servant / A. Pope

Address: To / The Revd. Dr Parnelle, / in / Dublin

20. Gay *to* Parnell[2] [*26 March 1716*]

Congleton MSS.

London, Monday

My Dear Parnelle, / I write this from Mr Lintots Shop where pray direct to me for the future, being just come to Town from Epsom with Dr Arbuthnot, but I was resolvd not to neglect a Post tho' I only shoud acquaint you with what I hope you knew before, that I love you, Pope I expect to town tonight from Binfield, where he has been these three or four days & now quits it for ever, nos Patriae fines & dulcia linquimus arva, I don't love Latin quotations but you

---

[1] Which Parnell had written for volume i of the *Iliad*.

[2] Reprinted, by permission, from C. J. Rawson's transcript of the original manuscript (*RES*, N.S. x [1959], 380–3). The original is badly deteriorated, making a photostatic copy virtually impossible to read. In addition to the evidence marshalled by Rawson for the authenticity of the Congleton copies

(*RES*, p. 371), one might also cite mannerisms in this letter characteristic of Gay's epistolary style: the byplay about not blotting the letter; the graceful compliment, '. . . I shoud only acquaint you with what you knew before, that I love you', which appears elsewhere in Gay's letters in variant form. The dating is by Rawson from internal evidence.

must consider him as a pastor[1] [and wri]ter. Binfield alas is
sold. the Trees of Windsor Forest shall no more listen to
the tunefull reed of the [?Popeian] swain & no more Beeches
shall be wounded with the names of Teresa & Patty. Teresa
& Patty too are forced to leave the Groves of Mapledurham
their Brother having forsaken a Mother [? & sisters &]
taken unto himself a wife, as Binfield is for ever sold when I
took my leave of Pope I recommended Bounce to his care
as he was a f[riend of his] and of yours. I believe you [   ]
humanity than to neglect [either] his dog or his friend, what
I got by walking the streets, I am now spending in riding in
Coaches & as I draw on the Bank but seldom & with much
caution I believe [I] will scarce break it. I was dissapointed
that you said nothing of your m[ice] & Frogs. as Ireland
curst the man that carried frogs first into it, so England is
no less disoblidged to you for carrying your Frogs from us.[2]
I have aimed att a Conceit, but since I writ it down find it is
a poor one, but I have taken a resolution not to blott my
letter. If you don't know what I mean lett us immediatly
appoint a meeti[ng] in England & I will Explain myself.

   The Miscellany that Pope mentiond is to be printed by
Lintot which will be publish'd I suppose if materials come
in, in a month or two.[3] I am oblidged to your Bookworm,[4]
now I talk of Worms I must just acquaint you of an odd
adventure that has lately happend att Buttons, some People
have lately taken a Whim of [mak]ing some of the Gentlemen
of that Coffee house void worms of a [? monstro]us size
[? for ad]vertisements by Mr John Moore's worm powder
[? which] as you are an advertisement reader you are undoubtedly acquainted with[.] the aforesaid Gentlemen are
Extreamly angry att this treatment & whenever Politicks
will give them leave the topick of their conversation is altogether upon worms a friend[5] [? or two] has writ this con-
gratulato[ry] Poem to Dr Moore

---

[1] i.e. shepherd, referring to Pope as
a pastoral writer.
   [2] Parnell took the manuscript of his
Batrachomuomachia to Ireland with him
in 1714, thus reversing the legendary
action of St. Patrick.
   [3] *Poems on Several Occasions* did not

reach print until 1717.
   [4] Parnell's poem, 'The Bookworm'.
   [5] Most certainly Pope. Pope never
publicly acknowledged authorship, but
both Sherburn and Ault attribute the
lines to him. See *Early Career*, p. 175;
Minor Poems, p. 163.

To the ingenious Mr John [Moore Author of the] celebrated Worm Powder

1

How much Egregious Moore are we
Decievd by Shows & Forms
What'eer we think, what'eer [we see,]
All human Race are worms

2

Man is a very worm by Birth
Vile Reptile, Proud & Vain.
Awhile he crawls upon the Earth
Then shrinks in Earth again

3

That Woman is a worm we find
E'er since our Grandam's Evil
She first conversed with her own kind
That ancient worm, the Devil

4

But whether [Man] or He, [God knows,]
Fecundifyed her [B]elly
With that pure stuff from whence we rose
The genial Vermicelli

5

The Learned themselves we Bookworms name
The Blockhead is a slow worm
The nymph whose tail is all on Flame
Is aptly termd, a Glow worm

6

The Fops are painted Butterflys
that flutter for a day
first from a worm they take their rise
And in a Worm decay.

7

The Flatterer an Earwig grows
Some worms suit all conditions
Misers are Muckworms, Silkworms Beaux
And Deathwatches Physicians

8
That Statesmen have the Worms is seen
By all their winding Play
Their conscience is a worm within
That gnaws them night & day

9
Ah Moore thy Skill were well Employed
    And Greater Gains woud rise
If thou coudst make the Courtier void
The worm that never dyes.

10
O Learned friend of Abchurch Lane
Who setts our Entrails free
Vain is thy Art, thy Powders vain
Since worms shall eat ev'n thee

11
Tho[u] only can[st our] fate adjourn
Some few short years no more
Ev'n Buttons Witts to w[orms shall] turn
Who Maggots were before

Sir R S. writ as I am informd the Preface with the
Assistance of Hoadly &c.[1] Mr Lintot publishd Oedipus
since & will send it.[2] lett the dean know that what I write to
you is Equal[ly] meant to him for no one loves you both
better / J Gay

21. Gay *to* Pope[3] [*January 1716/17*]

1745 (Ayre, *Memoirs of Pope*)

Dear Pope, / Too late I see, and confess myself mistaken,

[1] Parnell had evidently inquired
about the authorship of *An Account of
the State of the Roman Catholic Religion*
(1715). 'Sir R S.' is, of course, Steele.
Benjamin Hoadly (1676–1761), Bishop
of Bangor, whose sermon, 'Nature of the
Kingdom or Church of Christ' (1717),
precipitated the Bangorian Controversy,
is generally accepted as the author of
the Preface.

[2] Theobald's translation of Sophocles'
Oedipus.

[3] Dated from the references to *Three
Hours After Marriage,* written in

in Relation to the Comedy, yet I do not think had I follow'd your Advice, and only introduc'd the *Mummy*, that the Absence of the *Crocodile* had sav'd it. I can't help laughing myself, (though the Vulgar do not consider that it was design'd to look very ridiculous) to think how the poor Monster and Mummy were dash'd at their Reception, and when the Cry was loudest, thought that if the Thing had been wrote by another, I should have deem'd the Town in some Measure mistaken, and as to your Apprehension that this may do us future Injury, do not think it; the Doctor has a more valuable Name than can be hurt by any Thing of this Nature, and yours is doubly safe; I will (if any Shame there be) take it all to myself, as indeed I ought, the Motion being first mine, and never heartily approv'd of by you: As to what your early Enemy said at the Duke of *Dorset*'s and Mr. *Pulteney*'s, you will live to prove him a false Prophet, as you have already a Liar, and a Flatterer, and Poet in Spight of Nature; whether I shall do so or no, you can best tell, for with the Continuance of your dear Friendship and Assistance, never yet withheld from me, I dare promise as much.

I beg of you not to suffer this, or any Thing else, to hurt your Health. As I have publickly said, that I was assisted by two Friends, I shall still continue in the same Story, professing obstinate Silence about Dr. *Arbuthnot* and yourself. I am going Tomorrow to *Hampton Court* for a Week,[1] notwithstanding the Badness of the Weather, where, tho' I am to mix with Quality, I shall see nothing half so engaging as you my dear Friend.

I am (not at all cast down) | Your sincere Friend, | JOHN GAY.

collaboration with Pope and Arbuthnot, and produced at Drury Lane, 16 January 1717. For a detailed account of the play's uproarious reception, see George Sherburn, 'The Fortunes and Mis-fortunes of *Three Hours After Marriage*', *Modern Philology*, xxiv (1926), 91–109.

[1] Possibly to visit Mrs. Howard, Bedchamber Woman to Princess Caroline.

22. Gay, William *and* Ann Pulteney *to* Belladine¹
[*17 July 1717*]

Harvard University

My Dear Belladine
O're a Glass of Wine
We send you this line
On Purpose to tell
You & Miss Lepell²
We are all very well
If news we should send you from Canterbury
That news to be sure you would think is a lye
And therefore we'll say what before you did know
That we are Your Servants wherever we go.

> Ann Pulteney
> Wm. Pulteney.
> J Gay.

Canterbury. Saturday.

23. Gay *to* Mr. F——³ *9 August 1718*

1737 (*Letters of Mr. Alexander Pope*)

Stanton Harcourt, Aug. 9, 1718.

The only news you can expect to have from me here, is news from heaven, for I am quite out of the world, and there

¹ Mary Bellenden, Maid of Honour to Caroline, Princess of Wales.
   My dating is speculative. Gay and the Pulteneys set out for the Continent in mid July, 1717. See Pope to Parnell, 6 July [1717], *Pope Corr.* i. 416; see also *Favorite*, p. 167. This excursion undoubtedly provided the inspiration for Gay's *Epistle to the Right Honourable William Pulteney, Esq.* (1720). It is conceivable that the lines to 'Belladine' were penned by the trio while en route to the Channel ports and France. July 17 was

a Saturday in this year. The lines, most likely by Gay, are in Pulteney's hand but the signatures are autograph.
² Mary 'Molly' Lepell (1700–68), another of the Maids of Honour. In 1720 she married Lord Hervey.
³ This letter is known only from the version printed by Pope in the 1737 editions of his correspondence and is attributed to Gay solely on Pope's authority. Its similarity to Pope's account of the ill-fated lovers in his letter to Martha Blount, 6–9 August 1718

is scarce any thing can reach me except the noise of thunder, which undoubtedly you have heard too. We have read in old authors, of high towers levell'd by it to the ground, while the humble valleys escap'd: the only thing that is proof against it is the laurell which however I take to be no great security to the brains of modern authors. But to let you see that the contrary to this often happens, I must acquaint you, that the highest and most extravagant heap of towers in the universe, which is in this neighbourhood, stands still undefac'd, while a cock of barley in our next field has been consumed to ashes. Would to God that this heap of barley had been all that had perished! for unhappily beneath this little shelter sate two much more constant Lovers than ever were found in Romance under the shade of a beech-tree. John Hewet was a well-set man of about five and twenty; Sarah Drew might be rather called comely than beautiful, and was about the same age. They had pass'd thro' the various labours of the year together with the greatest satisfaction; if she milk'd, 'twas his morning and evening care to bring the cows to her hand; it was but last fair that he bought her a present of green silk for her straw hat, and the posie on her silver ring was of his choosing. Their love was the talk of the whole neighbourhood; for scandal never affirm'd that they had any other views than the lawful possession of each other in marriage. It was that very morning that he had obtain'd the consent of her parents, and it was but the next week that they were to wait to be happy. Perhaps in the intervals of their work they were now talking of the wedding cloaths, and John was suiting several sorts of poppys and field flowers to her complexion, to chuse her a knot for the wedding-day. While they were thus busied, (it was on the last of July between two or three in the afternoon) the clouds grew black, and such a storm of lightning and thunder ensued, that all the labourers made the best of their way to what shelter the trees and hedges afforded. Sarah was frightned, and fell down in a swoon on a heap of barley. John who never separated from

(*Pope Corr.* i. 479–82), is striking. Ayre identified 'Mr. F——' as Fenton (*Memoirs of Pope,* ii. 108) but if the letter was written by Gay, 'F——' is more likely to be Fortescue since there is no record of any correspondence between Gay and Fenton.

her, sate down by her side, having raked together two or three heaps the better to secure her from the storm. Immediately there was heard so loud a crack, as if heaven had split asunder; every one was now solicitous for the safety of his neighbour, and called to one another throughout the field. No answer being return'd to those who called to our Lovers, they stept to the place where they lay; they perceived the barley all in a smoak, and then spy'd this faithful pair; John with one arm about Sarah's neck, and the other held over her, as to skreen her from the lightning. They were struck dead, and stiffen'd in this tender posture. Sarah's left eye-brow was sing'd, and there appear'd a black spot on her breast; her Lover was all over black, but not the least signs of life were found in either. Attended by their melancholy companions, they were convey'd to the town, and the next day interr'd in Stanton-Harcourt Church-yard. My Lord Harcourt, at Mr. Pope's and my request, has caused a stone to be plac'd over them, upon condition that we furnish'd the Epitaph, which is as follows:

> When Eastern lovers feed the funeral fire;
> On the same pile the faithful fair expire;
> Here pitying heaven that virtue mutual found,
> And blasted both, that it might neither wound.
> Hearts so sincere th' Almighty saw well pleas'd,
> Sent his own lightning, and the Victims seiz'd.

But my Lord is apprehensive the country people will not understand this, and Mr Pope says he'll make one with something of scripture in it,[1] and with as little of poetry as Hopkins and Sternhold. / Your, &c.

24. Gay *to* Mrs. Howard *8 September 1719*

Add. 22626

Madam. / If it be absolutely necessary that I make an apology for my not writing, I must give you an account of

---

[1] For Pope's 'scriptural epitaph', see Pope to Lady Mary Wortley Montagu, 1 September [1718], *Pope Corr.* i. 495.

very bad Physicians, and a feaver which I had at Spaa that
confin'd me for a Month; but I dont see that I need make
the least excuse, or that I can find any reason for writing
to you at all, for can you believe that I would wish to converse with you, if it were not for the pleasure to hear you
talk again? then why should I write to you when there is no
possibility of receiving an Answer? I have been looking
every where since I came into France[1] to find out some
object that might take you from my thoughts, that my journey might seem less tedious, but since nothing could never
do it in England, I can much less expect it [in] France.

I am now rambling from Place to Place. In about a Month
I hope to be at Paris, and the next month to be in England,
and the next Minute to see you. I am now at Dijon in
Burgundy, where last night at an Ordinary I was surpris'd
by a Question from an English Gentleman whom I had never
seen before; hearing my name, he ask'd me, if I had any
relation or Acquaintance with myself and when I told him
I knew no such Person, he assur'd me that he was an
intimate acquaintance of Mr Gay at London. there was a
Scotch Gentleman who all supper time was teaching some
French Gentlemen the force and propriety of the English
Language, and what is seen very commonly, a young English
Gentleman with a Jacobite Governour. A French Marquis
drove an Abbé from the Table by railing against the vast
riches of the Church, and another Marquis who squinted,
endeavour'd to define Transubstantiation; that a thing might
not be what it really appear'd to be, my Eyes, says he, may
convince you, I seem at present to be looking on you, but
on the contrary I see quite on the other side of the table,
I dont believe that this Argument converted one of the
Hereticks present; for all that I learnt by him, was, that to
believe transubstantiation it is necessary not to look at the
thing you seem to look at. so much I have observ'd on the
Conversation & manners of the People, As for the Animals
of the Country; It abounds with Bugs, which are exceeding

---

[1] The circumstances of Gay's visit to the Continent in 1719 have never been satisfactorily explained. Irving specu- lates that Gay may have accompanied the Burlingtons in the capacity of secretary and travelling companion. See *Favorite*, p. 174.

familiar to Strangers; as for Plants, Garlick seems to be the favourite Plant of the Country, though for my own part I think the Vine preferable to it. when I publish my travells at Large I shall, be more particular, in order to which to morrow I set out for Lyons, from thence to Mompellier and so to Paris; and soon after I shall pray that the Winds may be favourable, I mean to bring you from Richmond to London, or me from London to Richmond, so prays / Madam / Your most obedient / Humble Servant / J Gay.

Dijon. Sepr. 8. NS. 1719.

I beg you, madam, to assure / Mrs Lepell & Mrs Ballenden / that I am their Humble / Servant.

25. Gay *to* Jacob Tonson, II[1] [*October 1720?*]

Add. 28275

Sir / I received your Letter with the accounts of the Books you had delivered,[2] I have not seen Mr Lintot's account but shall take the first opportunity to call upon him. I cannot think your Letter consists of the utmost civility, in five lines to press me twice to make up my account just at a time when it is impracticable to sell out of the Stocks in which my fortune is engag'd. between Mr Lintot & you the greatest part of the money is receiv'd; and I imagine you have a sufficient number of Books in your hands for the security of the rest. To go to the strictness of the matter, I own my note engages me to make the whole payment in the beginning of September, had it been in my power, I had not given you occasion to send to me, for I can assure you I am as impatient & uneasy to pay the money I owe, as some men are to receive it, and tis no small mortification to refuse you so reasonable

---

[1] The dating is, at best, a guess based on the fact that Gay was known to be in financial difficulties in the autumn of 1720, following the collapse of the South Sea Company. See *Favorite*, p. 186; see also *Poetical Works*, p. xxxvii.
[2] Gay's *Poems on Several Occasions*, published earlier in the year.

a request, which is, that I may no longer be obliged to you. /
I am Sir / your most humble Servant / J. Gay.

Friday morning.

26. Gay *to* Charles Lockyer[1] *24 February 1721*

The Huntington Library

Pay to Tho. Glegg my Dividend Due at Xtmas & Midsummer last on South Sea Stock, being 110 l and his Rescipt
shall be your Sufficient discharge. Feb. 24. 1721 / J Gay.
To Mr. Cha. Lockyer

27. Gay *to* [Charles Lockyer][2] *1 May 1721*

The Bodleian Library

May 1. 1721

Sir / Please to place to the Account of Alexander Pope
Esqr all such Stock as is due to me for one thousand pounds
of the third subscription paid in upon my Name for sale of
Southsea Stock / J Gay.

Endorsement: [On face of order in unknown hand] Mr. Gay-1000-3d
    fo: 1000

[1] Accountant for the South Sea
Company. With the exception of Gay's
signature, the draft is in another hand.
On the basis of this draft, and those of
1 May 1721 and 25 June 1722, both
Irving and Sherburn speculate that
Gay's losses in the South Sea Company
may not have been as complete as
Samuel Johnson and others have indicated. See *Favorite*, p. 186 and footnote;
see also *Pope Corr*. ii. 75, n. 5. However,
John Carswell, author of *The South Sea
Bubble* (1960), suggests that this is stock
assigned to Gay during the reorganiza-
tion of the Company, and the transfers
of dividends may represent payments on
loans which Gay had arranged during
the boom in order to buy stock.

[2] Sherburn identified the addressee of
this draft as Lockyer (*Pope Corr*. ii. 75).
The original (Montagu d. 1, f. 133r),
however, has only the salutation 'Sir',
and gives no addressee. If Sherburn's
identification was conjectural, it is, at
the same time, quite plausible since
Lockyer was then handling Gay's South
Sea transactions. See Letter 26.

28. Gay *to* Francis Colman[1] *23 August 1721*

1820 (*Posthumous Letters*)

My Dear Colman, / I hope you will believe me that Nobody interests himself more in your welfare than I do; I was mighty sorry I had not the opportunity of seeing you before you left England;[2] I wish you may find every thing to your advantage, & every thing agreeable; I own my not writing to you has the appearance of Forgetfullness, but there is no acquaintance you have thinks and talks of you oftener. you see I endeavour to persuade you into the same opinion of me, that you must be convinc'd I have of you, because I have, on many occasions, singled you from the rest of my Friends to confide in. I don't mention your happiness in Love, I wish you happiness in every thing beside. I hope Mrs. Colman[3] met with no difficultys in your journey; I am sure she will find none while she is with you. I live almost altogether with Lord Burlington and pass my time very agreeably. I left Cheswick about three weeks ago, and have been ever since at the Bath for the Cholical humour in my stomach that you have heard me often complain off; Here is very little Company that I know; I expect a summons very suddenly to go with Lord Burlington into Yorkshire. you must think that I cannot be now and then without some thoughts that give me uneasiness, who have not the least prospect of ever being independent; my Friends do a great deal for me, but I think I could do more for them. Mr. Pulteney & Mrs. Pulteney had some thoughts of the Bath, but I fancy their journey is put off; I saw them at Cheswick just before I left it. you'l hear before my Letter can reach you of poor Lord Warwick's death;[4] it has given me many a melancholy reflection; I lov'd him, and cannot help feeling concern whenever I think of him. Dear Colman be as cheerfull

---

[1] Diplomat, literary and musical dilettante, and father of George Colman the Elder.

[2] For Florence, where Colman had been appointed British Resident.

[3] *Née* Mary Gumley, sister of Ann Pulteney.

[4] Edward Henry Rich, 7th Earl of Warwick and Addison's stepson. According to GEC, XII. ii. 418, Warwick died of a fever on 16 August 1721, 'having killed himself with his debauchery'.

as you can, never sink under a disappointment, I give you the advice which I have always endeavourd to follow, though I hope you will have no occasion to practise it; for I heartily wish you may be always cheerfull; and that you may always have very good reasons to be so. / I am / Dear Colman, / Yours most sincerely. / J. GAY.

Bath, Aug. 23, 1721.

My service to Mrs. Colman—direct to me at White's, if you will give me the pleasure of hearing from you.

29. Gay *to* Conrad de Gols[1] *25 June 1722*

The Historical Society of Pennsylvania

June 25th 1722.

Sir / I desire you will pay to Mr Henry Watson the Dividend on all my Stock in Your Books due at Christmas last past and his Receipt shall be a Sufficient discharge from / Sir / Your most humble / Servant. / J Gay.

To / Canrade D'Gols Esqr. / Cashier to the South / Sea Company

30. Gay *to* Swift *22 December 1722*

Add. 4805

Dear Sir. / After every post-day for these 8 or 9 years I have been troubled with an uneasiness of Spirit, and at last I have resolv'd to get rid of it and write to you;[2] I dont deserve that you should think so well of me as I really deserve, for I have not profest to you that I love you as much as ever I did, but you are the only person of my acquaintance

---

[1] An official of the Bank of England, de Gols was brought in after the collapse to help straighten out the Company's affairs.

[2] Gay had evidently not written to

Swift since 16 August 1714. The reader will recognize, in Gay's complaints, the echoes of his letter to Francis Colman, 23 August 1721 (Letter 28).

almost that does not know it. Whoever I see that comes from Ireland, the first Question I ask is after your health, of which I had the pleasure to hear very lately from Mr Berkeley.[1] I think of you very often, no body wishes you better, or longs more to see you. Duke Disney[2] who knows more news than any man alive, told me I should certainly meet you at the Bath the last Season, but I had one comfort in being disappointed that you did not want it for your health; I was there for near eleven weeks for a Cholick that I have been troubled with of late, but have not found all the benefit I expected. I lodge at present in Burlington house,[3] and have received many Civilitys from many great men but very few real benefits. They wonder at each other for not providing for me, and I wonder at 'em all. Experience has given me some knowledge of them, so that I can say that tis not in their power to dissappoint me. You find I talk to you of myself, I wish you would reply in the same manner. I hope though you have not heard from me so long I have not lost my Credit with you, but that you will think of me in the same manner as when you espous'd my cause so warmly which my gratitude never can forget. / I am / Dear Sir / Your most obliged & / Sincere humble Servant / J Gay.

London. Decemr. 22. 1722.

Mr Pope upon reading over / this Letter desir'd me to tell / you that he has been just in / the same Sentiments with me / in regard to you, and shall never / forget his obligations to you.

Address: To / The Revd. Dr Swift Dean of / St Patrick's in / Dublin. Ireland.

Endorsements: [In Swift's hand] Mr Gay / Decb. 22d. 1722
Mr Gay / Rx Decb 28th 1722

[1] George Berkeley (1685–1735), the philosopher.
[2] Henry Desaulnais, a French Huguenot who had Anglicized his name, was at this time a retired army officer. He was a member of the Brothers' Club and an early friend of Bolingbroke and the Tory Wits. He acquired the sobriquet 'Duke' from his habit of using the word as an ejaculation. See Gay's *Mr. Pope's Welcome from Greece*, 29–32.
[3] Gay resided at Burlington House and in his apartment at Whitehall until 1728, when he moved to the Queensberrys' estate at Amesbury in Wiltshire, where he spent the greater part of his remaining years.

31. Gay *to* Swift *3 February 1722/3*

Add. 4805

You made me very happy by answering my Letter in so
kind a manner, which to common appearance I did not
deserve, but I believe you guess'd my thoughts, and knew
that I had not forgot you, and that I always lov'd you. When
I found that my Book was not sent to you by Tooke,[1] Jervas
undertook it, and gave it to Mr Maxwell who married a
neice of Mr Meredith's. I am surpris'd you have heard
nothing of it, but Jervas has promis'd me to write about it,
so that I hope you will have it delivered to you soon. Mr
Congreve I see often, he always mentions you with the
strongest expressions of esteem and friendship, he labours
still under the same afflictions as to his Sight and Gout, but
in his intervals of Health, he has not lost any thing of his
Cheerfull temper; I pass'd all the last Season with him at the
Bath, and I have great reason to value myself upon his
friendship, for I am sure he sincerely wishes me well. we
pleas'd ourselves with the thoughts of seeing you there, but
Duke Disney, who knows more intelligence than any body
besides, chanc'd to give us a wrong information. If you had
been there, the Duke promis'd, upon my giving him notice,
to make you a visit; he often talks of you, & wishes to see
you. I was two or three days ago at Dr Arbuthnot's who told
me he had writ you three Letters, but had receiv'd no answer.
He chargd me to send you his advice; which is, to come to
England, and see your friends, this he affirms (abstracted
from the desire he has to see you) to be very good for your
health. he thinks that your going to Spa, and drinking the
waters there would be of great service to you, if you have
resolution enough to undertake the journey. But he would
have you try England first. I like the prescription very much,
but I own I have a self interest in it, for your taking this

---

[1] In his reply to Gay's letter of
22 December 1722 (Letter 30), Swift
had complained that he had not received
a copy of Gay's *Poems on Several
Occasions* (1720). Benjamin Tooke Jr.,
son of Swift's former publisher and
financial agent, had succeeded to the
business on the death of his father in
1716. See *Journal*, i. 13, n. 11.

journey would certainly do me a great deal of good. Pope has just now embark'd himself in another great undertaking as an Author, for of late he has talk'd only as a Gardiner.[1] He has engag'd to translate the Odyssey in three years, I believe rather out of a prospect of Gain than inclination, for I am persuaded he bore his part in the loss of the Southsea. He lives mostly at Twickenham, and amuses himself in his house and Garden. I supp'd about a fortnight ago with Lord Bathurst & Lewis at Dr Arbuthnot's, whenever your old acquaintance meet they never fail of expressing their want of you. I wish you would come & be convinc'd that all I tell you is true. As for the reigning Amusement of the town, tis entirely Musick. real fiddles, Bass Viols and Hautboys not poetical Harps, Lyres, and reeds. Theres nobody allow'd to say I sing but an Eunuch or an Italian Woman. Every body is grown now as great a judge of Musick as they were in your time of Poetry. and folks that could not distinguish one tune from another now daily dispute about the different Styles of Hendel, Bononcini, and Attillio. People have now forgot Homer, and Virgil & Caesar, or at least they have lost their ranks, for in London and Westminster in all polite conversation's Senesino is daily voted to be the greatest man that ever liv'd. I am oblig'd to you for your advice, as I have been formerly for your assistance in introducing me into Business. I shall this year be a commissioner of the State Lottery which will be worth to me a hundred & fifty pounds; and I am not without hopes that I have friends that will think of some better & more certain provision for me. you see I talk to you of myself as a thing of consequence to you. I judge by myself, for to hear of your health, and happiness will always be one of my greatest satisfactions. Every one that I have nam'd in the Letter give their Service to you, I beg you give mine, Mr Popes, & Mr Kent's[2] to Mr Ford. / I am / Dear Sir / Your most faithfull / Humble Servant / JG.

London. Febr. 3. 1722/3.

[1] Pope had been occupied for nearly four years with the remodelling and landscaping at Twickenham. The celebrated grotto was completed the previous summer. See *Early Career,* pp. 270–305.

[2] William Kent (1684–1748), 'painter, sculptor, architect, and landscape gardener'. See *DNB* entry. He was, like Gay, a protégé of the Burlingtons.

[On verso]: My paper was so thin / that I was forc'd to / make use of a cover / I do not require the / like Civility in return.

Endorsement: Mr Gay / Feb. 3d—1722-3 [Swift's hand]

32. Gay *to* Mrs. Howard *12 July 1723*

Add. 22626

Tunbridge. July. 12. 1723.[1]

Madam / The next pleasure to seeing of you is hearing from you, and when I hear you succeed in your wishes, I succeed in mine, so I will not say a word more of the house.[2] We have a Lady here that is very particular in her desires. I have known some Ladys who (if ever they prayd and were sure their prayers would prevail) would ask an Equipage, a Title, a husband, or Matadores, but this Lady who is but seventeen, and has but thirty thousand pound has all her wishes in a pot of good ale. when her friends for the sake of her shape & complexion would dissuade her from it, she answers with the truest sincerity, that by the loss of shape & complexion she can only lose a husband, but that Ale is her taste. I have not as yet drank with her, though I must own I cannot help being fond of a Lady who has so little disguise of her practice either in her words or appearance. If to show you love her, you must drink with her, she has chose an ill place for followers, for she is forbid with the waters. Her shape is not very unlike a Barrel, and I would describe her Eyes, if I could look over the agreeable swellings of her cheeks in which the rose predominates, nor can I perceive the least of the Lilly in her whole countenance. You see what thirty thousand pounds can do, for without that I could never have discover'd all these agreeable particularitys. in short, she is the Ortolan, or rather wheat-ear[3] of the place for she is

---

[1] Gay had accompanied the Countess of Burlington to Tunbridge. See Pope to Gay, 13 July 1723, *Pope Corr*. ii. 181.

[2] Marble Hill, the villa at Twickenham which the Prince of Wales was building for her.

[3] Ortolan—a small singing bird, a species of bunting or finch; Wheatear—small bird of the thrush family, the name of which is a corruption of *whiters* (= 'white rump'). As early as 1653 an association with wheat was made, in

entirely a lump of fat, and the form of the Universe itself is scarce more beautifull, for her figure is almost circular. after I have said all this, I believe 'twill be in vain for me to declare I am not in love and I am afraid that I have show'd some imprudence in talking upon this subject, since you have declar'd that you like a friend that has a heart in his disposal. I assure you, I am not mercenary, and that thirty thousand pounds has not half so much power with me as the woman I love.

33. Gay *to* Mrs. Howard[1] [*August 1723*]

Add. 22626

I have long wish'd to be able to put in practice that valuable worldly qualification of being insincere, one of my cheif reasons is that I hate to be particular, and I think if a man cannot conform to the customs of the world, he is not fit to be encourag'd or to live in it. I know that if one would be agreeable to men of dignity one must study to imitate them, and I know which way they get Money and places. I cannot indeed wonder that the Talents requisite for a great Statesman are so scarce in the world since so many of those who possess them are every month cut off in the prime of their Age at the Old-Bailý.[2] How envious are Statesmen! and how jealous are they of rivals! A Highway-man never picks up an honest man for a companion, but if such a one accidentally falls in his way; if he cannot turn his heart He like a wise Statesman discards him. Another observation I have made upon Courtiers, is, that if you have any friendship with any particular one you must be entirely govern'd by his friendships and resentments not your own, you are not only to flatter him but those that he flatters, and if he chances to take a fancy to [a] man whom you know that he knows to have the Talents of a Statesman you are immediately to think both of

that the wheatear is fattest when the wheat, on which it feeds, is ripe. See *NED*. Both were esteemed as table delicacies in the eighteenth century.

[1] The dating is based on internal evidence indicating that this letter is a reply to Mrs. Howard's of 22 July [1723].

[2] An early suggestion of the format of *The Beggar's Opera*.

them men of the most exact Honour. in short, you must think nothing dishonest or dishonourable that is requir'd of you, because if you know the world you must know that no Statesman has or ever will require any thing of you that is dishonest or dishonourable. Then you must suppose that all Statesmen, and your friend in particular, (for Statesmen's friends have always seem'd to think so) have been, are, and always will be guided by strict justice, and are quite void of partiality and resentment. You are to believe that he never did or can propose any wrong thing, for whoever has it in his power to dissent from a Statesman in any one particular, is not capable of his friendship. this last word friendship I have been forc'd to make use of several times though I know that I speak improperly for it has never been allow'd a Court term. This is some part of a Court Creed, though it is impossible to fix all the Articles. for as men of Dignity believe one thing one day, and another the next, so you must daily change your faith and opinion. therefore the method to please these wonderfull and mighty men, is never to declare in the morning what you believe 'till your friend has declar'd what he believes, for one mistake this way is utter destruction. I hope these few reflections will convince you that I know something of the Art of pleasing great men. I have strictly examin'd most favourites that I have known, and think I judge right, that almost all of them have practic'd most of these rules in their way to perferment. I cannot wonder that great men require all this from their Creatures, since most of them have practic'd it themselves, or else they had never arriv'd to their dignitys.[1]

As to your advice that you give me in relation to preaching & marrying, and Ale, I like it extreamly, for this Lady must be born to be a Parson's wife, and I never will think of marrying her till I have preach'd my first sermon.[2] She was last night at a Private Ball, so private that not one man knew it 'till 'twas over, so that Mrs Carr was disturb'd at her

---

[1] Gay's fit of philosophizing was prompted by Mrs. Howard's expressed fear that Gay was inclined to be too candid and trusting. There is something ludicrous about John Gay's lecturing Mrs. Howard on how to get along at Court.

[2] Mrs. Howard had suggested that Gay was as likely to marry his plump 'wheat-ear' as he was to turn parson. See Mrs. Howard to Gay, 22 July [1723], *Suffolk Corr.* i. 110.

Lodgings by only a dozen Ladys, who danc'd together without the least scandal. I fancy I shall not stay here much longer, though what will become of me I know not, for I have not and fear never shall have a will of my own.

34. Gay *to* Mrs. Howard¹ [*September 1724*]

Add. 22626

Madam./ Since I came to the Bath I have writ three Letters. The first to you, the second to Mr Pope, and the third to Mr Fortescue.² Every Post gives me fresh mortification, for I am forgot by every body. Dr Arbuthnot & his Brother went away this morning, & intend to see Oxford in their way to London. The talk of the Bath is the marriage of Lord Sommerville & Mrs Rolt, she left the Bath Yesterday, he continues here, but is to go away to day or to morrow. but as opinions differ, I cannot decide whether they are married or no. Lord Essex gives a private Ball in Harrison's great Room to Mrs Pelham this evening, so that in all probability some odd Bodys, being left out we shall soon have the pleasure of being divided into Factions. I shall return to London with Lord Scarborough, who hath not as yet fixt his time of leaving the Bath. Lord Fitz-Williams this morning had an account a Ticket of his was come up 500. Lady Fitz-Williams wonders she has not heard from you, and has so little resolution that she cannot resist Butter'd Rolls at Breakfast, though she knows they prejudice her health. If you will write to me you will make me chearfull & happy, with out which I am told the waters will have no good effect. pray, have some regard to my health, for my Life is at your Service.

---

¹ Dated from Gay's reference to the marriage of James Lord Somerville to Mrs. Anne Rolt, which took place at Bath, 18 September 1724. See GEC, XII. i. 105.

² Gay went to Bath with Arbuthnot in mid September 1724. See Pope to Fortescue, 17 September 1724, *Pope Corr.* ii. 257. The letters to Pope and Fortescue which Gay mentions are lost.

35. Gay *to* Pope¹ [*2 September 1725*]

Homer MSS. Add. 4809

Dear Sir / I can neglect no opportunity that can give you Satisfaction or pleasure. I this instant came from Dr Arbuthnot, & I hope found him reliev'd from all the danger of his distemper; about an hour or two ago, he made water & had a stool, and, is quite free from pain. He is weak, & very much reduc'd, but Amiens² whom I found with him thinks him out of danger. I shall dine at Petersum³ on Sunday, & intend to see Mrs Howard; From Petersum we set out for Wiltshire on Monday. pray give my sincere service to Mrs Pope, & Mrs Blount. / I am / Dear Sir / Yours most affectionately / JG. Thursday. / 10 at night.

Postmark: 2/SE

36. Gay *and* Pope *to* Fortescue *23 September 1725*

1817 (*Original Letters*)

Sept. 23, 1725.

DEAR SIR, / I am again returned to Twickenham, upon the news of the person's death you wrote to me about.⁴ I cannot say I have any great prospect of success; but the affair remains yet undetermined, and I cannot tell who will be his

---

¹ Dated from the postmark and Gay's remark that he is writing 'Thursday / 10 at night'. 2 September in 1725, was a Thursday. The year is established by Arbuthnot's illness, which occurred in the late summer of 1725. See Pope to Swift, 14 September 1725, *Pope Corr*. ii. 322; see also Letter 36.

² Claude Amyand, surgeon and Fellow of the Royal Society. He was Master of the United Company of Barber-Surgeons in 1731. See Sidney Young, *Annals of the Barber-Surgeons of London* (1890), pp. 565–7; see also R. S. Cobbett, *Memorials of Twicken-*

ham (1872), p. 57. R. S. Walker identifies Amyand's son, Claudius, with the 'Mr. Amiot' to whom Mrs. Montagu introduced Dr. Beattie on 22 May 1773. See *James Beattie's London Diary* (1946), pp. 39, 113.

³ Petersham, where Gay was to join the Queensberrys for the trip to Amesbury.

⁴ From his visit to Wiltshire with the Queensberrys. Fortescue's news that an appointment might be available brought Gay scurrying back to London. As usual, his hopes came to naught. See *Favorite*, p. 210; see also Letter 38.

successor. I know I have sincerely your good wishes upon all occasions. One would think that my friends use me to disappointments, to try how many I could bear; if they do so, they are mistaken; for as I don't expect much, I can never be much disappointed. I am in hopes of seeing you in town the beginning of October, by what you writ to Mr. Pope; and sure your father[1] will think it reasonable that Miss Fortescue should not forget her French and dancing. Dr. Arbuthnot has been at the point of death by a severe fit of illness, an imposthumation in the bowels; it hath broke, and he is now pretty well recovered. I have not seen him since my return from Wiltshire, but intend to go to town the latter end of the week.

I have made your compliments to Mrs. Howard this morning: she indeed put me in mind of it, by enquiring after you. Pray make my compliments to your sisters and Mrs. Fortescue; Mr. Pope desires the same.

Your's, most affectionately, / J. G.

'Blessed is the man who expects nothing, for he shall never be disappointed,' was the ninth beatitude which a man of wit (who, like a man of wit, was a long time in gaol) added to the eighth; I have long ago preached this to our friend; I have *preached* it, but the world and his other friends *held it forth*, and exemplified it. They say, Mr. Walpole has friendship, and keeps his word; I wish he were our friend's friend, or had ever promised him any thing.

You seem inquisitive of what passed when Lord Peterborow spirited him[2] hither, without any suspicion of mine. Nothing extraordinary, for the most extraordinary men are nothing before their masters; and nothing, but that Mr. Walpole swore by G-D, Mrs. Howard should have the grounds she wanted from V———n.[3] Nothing would be more

[1] No doubt a misreading in the transcript of 'ye' for 'yr'. Gay means 'the' father, i.e. Fortescue himself, as Sherburn has suggested (*Pope Corr.* ii. 322, n. 4).

[2] Walpole. Sherburn speculates (*Pope Corr.* ii. 323, n. 1) that the first reference is to Horatio Walpole, the Prime Minis-

ter's brother, but it seems evident that Pope is referring to Sir Robert throughout.

[3] Sir Thomas Vernon of Twickenham Park apparently owned land which Mrs. Howard wanted in order to enlarge Marble Hill. See Cobbett, *Memorials of Twickenham*, pp. 231, 235.

extraordinary, except a statesman made good his promise or oath, (as very probably he will.) If I have any other very extraordinary thing to tell you, it is this, that I have never since returned Sir R. W.'s visit. The truth is, I have nothing to ask of him; and I believe he knows that nobody follows him *for nothing*. Besides, I have been very sick, and sickness (let me tell you) makes one above a minister, who cannot cure a fit of a fever or ague. Let me also tell you, that no man who is lame, and cannot stir, will wait upon the greatest man upon earth; and lame I was, and still am, by an accident which it will be time enough to tell you when we meet,[1] for I hope it will be suddenly. Adieu, dear Sir, and believe me a true well-wisher to all your's, and ever your faithful, affectionate servant, / A. POPE.

Twitenham, Sept. 23, 1725.

Address: *To* WM. FORTESCUE, *esq; at Fallapit, near* / *Totnes, Devon.*

37. Gay *to* Pope[2] [*September 1725*]

Homer MSS. Add. 4809

Saturday night

Dear Sir. / I really intended to have been with you to day, but having been dissappointed yesterday of meeting Mr Selwyn;[3] & going to the Exchequer about my Salary[4] to day, & to Mrs Howard's to meet him made it too late, so that I made a visit this morning to Mr Congreve, where I found Lord Cobham they both enquir'd kindly for you & wish'd to see you soon, Mr Fortescue could not have come with me but intends the latter end of next week to see you at Twickenham. I have seen our Friend Dean Berkeley who was very solicitous about your health & welfare. He is now so full of

[1] Pope's 'accident' is something of a mystery. He speaks of a fever incurred during the summer in several letters (to Oxford, 7 September; to Edward Blount, 13 September) but this is the only mention of an accident.

[2] Dated from its chronological posi-tion in the Homer MSS. The letter, 'writ to you yesterday', of which Gay speaks is apparently lost.

[3] Col. John Selwyn, Groom of the Bedchamber to the Prince of Wales.

[4] As Commissioner of the Lottery, a post which Gay held 1723–31.

his Bermuda's project[1] that he hath printed his Proposal, and hath been with the Bishop of London about it. Mrs Howard desir'd me to tell you that she hath had a present of Beech Mast which this year hath been particularly good. when tis wanted she would have you send to her. I writ to you yesterday; and am in hopes that Mrs Pope will soon be so well that you may be able to come to town for a day or so about your business. I really am this evening very much out of order with the Cholick but I hope a night's rest will relieve me. I wish Mrs Pope & you all health & happiness, pray give my service to her.

38. Gay *to* Brigadier James Dormer[2] *30 October 1725*

Rousham MSS.

Dear Brigadier / There is never a day passes but I think of you & wish to see you; I have made all the enquiry I possibly could of your Welfare, but have been able to get very little intelligence; I believe you will think me sincere when I tell you that next to being witness that you are happy, one of the greatest satisfactions I could have, is to hear you are so. I hope I have no occasion to make any professions of friendship to you, because I have really more of it than I can profess; so that I shall only think of giving you an account of your friends & among those myself in the remaining part of my Letter. Mrs Pulteney is brought to bed of a son; they are both very well, & Mr Pulteney is the happiest man alive, Lord & Lady Burlington are return'd to Cheswick from Yorkshire. Kent is employ'd in making vast Alterations in Newcastle-house in Lincoln's Inn fields. I din'd with him to day at Williams his Coffee-house, & he left me in order to pass his Sunday as usual at Cheswick. Mr Pelham came to town Yesterday for the Birthday to day from the Duke of Graftons; as did several others of the Court, who will leave

---

[1] Berkeley was then in London seeking support for his scheme of establishing a college in Bermuda. See A. A. Luce, *Life of Berkeley* (1949), pp. 97 ff.

[2] James Dormer (1679–1741), later Lieutenant-General, an early friend and patron of Gay's. He was one of the pall-bearers at Gay's funeral in 1732.

us again in a day or two. Faustina[1] is engag'd to be here in the spring and is to have a Benefit day for her performance the latter part of this season[,] & is at a certain salary for the next year. By what I hear, I think the King is not expected till after Christmas. I have been this summer at Amesbury with the Duke of Queensberry; I came away from thence Post upon one of my usual prospects, & met with my usual success, a dissappointment.[2] I have employ'd myself this summer in study, & have made a progress in it. What I am about is a Book of Fables, which I hope to have leave to inscribe to Prince William. I design to write fifty, all entirely new, in the same sort of verse as Prior's tales. I have already done about forty, but as yet there are very few of my friends know of my intention. The Duke of Queensberry is not yet come to town, but I intend to go no more into the Country this Winter. Duke Disney hath for this month or two past had a severe fit of illness, but is now pretty well recover'd; he is going to leave his Lodgings at Whitehall into a house in St Jame's place, & I have some prospect of getting them. The town is at present so very thin that I am forc'd to write you all these most important things of myself. I beg you upon all occasions if I can be of any service to you to make use of me with the greatest freedom, for it will be the greatest pleasure to me to have your Commands. I am / Dear Sir / Your most obedient & faith / full Servant J Gay.

London / Octr. 30. 1725.

39. Gay *to* The Countess of Burlington[3]

28 August 1726

Yale University

Madam. / Whenever I have the opportunity of showing respect to your Ladyship, I cannot let it slip, so that I take the first occasion of writing to you, for I had rather do more than you expect from me, than omit doing what I think I

---

[1] Faustina Bordoni, a popular operatic singer.

[2] See also Letter 36.

[3] Hitherto unknown, this would appear to be the only letter extant from Gay to the Burlingtons.

ought to do. I had not the opportunity of wishing your Ladyship a good Voyage, but my Lord & your Ladyship always have my good wishes though they are not made in forms. I have had the pleasure to hear that your passage from Dover to Calais was perform'd in a few hours and without danger, I wish, after much pleasure, your return may be the same. I write this Letter on Sunday night while I imagine you to be at the Opera. How poorly are we oblig'd to entertain ourselves! for Kent[1] and I thought ourselves very happy on Friday night with Bartholomew Fair and the Siege of Troy.[2] I think the Poet corrected Virgil with great judgment in the Poetical justice which he observ'd; for Paris was kill'd upon the spot by Menelaus, and Helen burnt in the flames of the town before the Audience. The Trojan Horse was large [as] life and extreamly well painted; the sight of which struck Kent with such astonishment, that he prevaild with me to go with him the next day to compare it with the celebrated paintings at Greenwich.[3] Kent did not care to reflect upon a Brother of the Pencil; but if I can make any judgment from hums, & hahs, and little hints, he seem'd to give the preference to Bartholomew Fair. For my own part, I was in concern that the show-man did Sir James Cornhill (as he call'd him) so much injustice for he pointed out to us Four Cardinals near King William, which he called the four Cardinals of Virtue. Which seem'd to me to include some Absurditys; in the first place, that there should be four Cardinals of Virtue in being; & that there should be four Cardinals attending a Protestant Prince. I inform'd the man that his account tended much to the prejudice of Sir James, that though they might appear four Cardinals to him, the Painter certainly

[1] Kent was most likely living in his apartments at Burlington House while engaged in renovating Kensin on Palace.

[2] By Elkanah Settle.

[3] The Painted Hall at the Royal Hospital, Greenwich, now the Officers' Mess of the Royal Naval College. The artist, Sir James Thornhill (1675–1734), the first great English 'history-painter', devoted twenty years (1707–27) to executing the scenes and figures from history and allegory which decorate the walls and ceilings of the Hall. See Sir Richard Steele's account of the paintings in *The Lover*, No. 33, Tuesday, 11 May 1714; see also Thornhill's *An Explanation of the Painting in the Royal Hospital at Greenwich* (1727).

Thornhill and Kent were at odds over Kent's employment at Kensington Palace, which Sir James, as Serjeant-Painter to the King, felt was his prerogative. The Burlingtons, of course, championed Kent.

meant them to express the four Cardinal Virtues. He then show'd us the Princess of Savoy, and the Queen of Persia, Here again I interrupted him, by telling him, that they might indeed be more like those two Ladys, but that certainly Sir James meant them for the Princess Sophia and the Queen of Prussia. This is a proof that a fine puppet-show may be spoild and depreciated by an ignorant interpreter. Mr Pulteney is return'd to Thistleworth[1] in good health, I intend to see him to morrow. If there was anybody in town I should not talk so much of myself and of consequence should have materials of better entertaining you. If your Ladyship thinks I have not done a work of supererrogation in writing to you I know you will honour me with [an] answer. I am / Madam, / Your Ladyship's & my Lord's most / obedient & most faithfull Servant / J Gay.

I beg my compliments to / Sir Harry.

London Aug. 28. 1726.

Address: A Madame / Madame la Comtesse de Burlington / a Paris / France

40. Gay *to* Swift *16 September 1726*

Add. 4805

Dear Sir. / Since I wrote last I have been always upon the ramble; I have been in Oxfordshire with the Duke & Dutchess of Queensberry, and at Petersum & wheresoever they would carry me; but as they will go to Wiltshire without me on tuesday next for two or three months, I believe I shall then have finish'd my travells for this Year, & shall not go farther from London than now & then to Twickenham. I saw Mr Pope on Sunday, who hath lately escap'd a very great danger, but is very much wounded across his right hand; Coming home in the dark about a week ago alone in my Lord Bolingbroke's coach from Dawley,[2] he was overturn'd where a bridge had been broken down near Whitton about a mile

---

[1] An older form of Isleworth.
[2] Bolingbroke's estate in Middlesex, four miles from Twickenham.

from his own house, he was thrown into the river with the
glasses of the coach up, & was up to the knots of his perriwig
in water; The footman broke the glass to draw him out, by
which he thinks he received the cut across his hand. He was
afraid he should have lost the use of his little finger & the
next to it; but the surgeon whom he sent for last Sunday
from London to examine it, told him, that his fingers were
safe, that there were two nerves cut, but no tendon. He is in
very good health, & very good spirits, and the wound in a
fair way of being soon heal'd.[1] The instructions you sent me
to communicate to the Doctor about the Singer, I transcrib'd
from your own Letter[2] and sent to him, for at that time he
was going every other day to Windsor park to visit Mr
Congreve who hath been extreamly ill, but is now recovered,
so that I was prevented from seeing of him by going out of
town myself. I din'd & sup'd on Monday last with Lord &
Lady Bolingbroke at Lord Berkeley's at Cranford & return'd
to London with the Duke & Dutchess of Queensberry on
tuesday by two a Clock in the morning, you are remember'd
always with great respect by all your acquaintance, and
every one of them wishes for your return. The Lottery begins
to be drawn on Monday next, but my week of attendance
will be the first in October.[3] I am oblig'd to follow the Gravers
to make them dispatch my plates for the Fables, for, without
it I find they proceed but very slowly. I take your advice in
this, as I wish to do in all things, and frequently revise my
work in order to finish it as well as I can. Mr Pulteney takes
the Letter you sent him in the kindest manner, and I believe
he is, except a few excursions, fixt in town for the winter. As
for the particular affair that you want to be inform'd in, we
are as yet wholy in the dark, but Mr Pope will follow your
instructions.[4] Mr Lancelot[5] sent for the Spectacles you left

---

[1] While Pope was handicapped by his
injury, Gay, and perhaps others, served
as his amanuensis. See Letter 42; see also
the 'Receipt for Stewing Veal' below.

[2] During his stay in England Swift
assumed a note for five guineas which
'Fox the Singer' had given to Arbuthnot. See Swift to Gay, 28 March 1728,
Swift Corr. iii. 277. The letter contain-
ing Swift's instructions has been lost.

[3] As Commissioner of the Lottery.

[4] The 'affair' is most likely the publication of *Gulliver's Travels* which
appeared the following month.

[5] William ? Lancelot, a servant of the
Earl of Sussex and second husband of
Swift's 'cousin', Patty Rolt. For a
detailed account of the complex relation-
ship of Swift to his 'cousins', see *Journal*,
i. 18, n. 26 and 72, n. 30.

behind you, which were deliver'd to him, Mr Jervas's sheets
are sent home to him mended, finely wash'd, & neatly folded
up.¹ I intend to see Mr Pope to morrow or on Sunday. I
have not seen Mrs Howard a great while, which you know
must be a great mortification & self-denial, but in my case
'tis particularly unhappy that a man cannot contrive to be in
two places at the same time; If I could, while you are there,
one of them should be always Dublin. but after all, tis a Silly
thing to be with a friend by halves, so that I will give up all
thoughts of bringing this project to perfection, if you will
contrive that we shall meet again soon. I am / Dear Sir /
Your most oblig'd & affectionate / friend & Servant J G.
London Sept. 16. 1726.

Address: To / The Revd Dr Swift Dean of / St Patricks in / Dublin. /
  Ireland
Postmark: 17/SE
Endorsement: Mr Gay / Sept. 16. 1726 [Swift's hand]

41. Gay *to* Swift² [*September 1726*]

Add. 4805

As We cannot enjoy any good thing without your par-
taking of it. Accept of the following receipt for Stewing Veal.
Take a knuckle of Veal,
You may buy it, or steal,
In a few peices cut it,
In a Stewing pan put it,
Salt, pepper and mace
Must season this Knuckle,
Then what's join'd to a place,¹   ¹Vulg. Salary.
With other Herbs muckle;

---

¹ Gay had borrowed some extra sheets
from Jervas while Swift was staying in
his apartment at Whitehall. See also
Letter 50.

² Originally part of a joint letter from
Pope, Gay, Bolingbroke, Mrs. Howard,
Pulteney, and Arbuthnot. Bolingbroke
called it a 'Cheddar letter' (Bolingbroke
to Swift, 22 September 1726, *Swift*

Corr. iii. 167), on the analogy of several
dairies contributing to a cheddar cheese,
and the dating is based on this reference.
The 'Receipt', the only portion of the
letter to survive, is undoubtedly by
Pope, and is in Gay's hand only because
of Pope's injury in the coach accident.
See Ault, *New Light*, pp. 225–30; see
also *Minor Poems*, pp. 253–5.

That which killed King Will,[2]   [2]Suppos'd sorrell
And what never stands still[3]   [3]This is by Dr / Bentley
Some sprigs of that bed[4]   thought to be / Time, or
Where Children are bred,   Thyme.
Which much you will mend, if   [4]Parsley. Vide Cham/ber-
Both Spinnage and Endive,   lain.
And Lettuce and Beet,
With Marygold meet;
Put no water at all;
For it maketh things small:
Which, lest it should happen,
A close cover clap on;
Put this pot of[5] Wood's mettle   [5]of this com/position see
In a hot boiling kettle,   the Work / of the Copper
And there let it be,   farthing / Dean.
(Mark the doctrine I teach)
About—let me see,—
Thrice as long as you[6] preach.   [6]Which we suppose to be
So skimming the fat off,   near / four hours.
Say Grace with your hat off,
O then, with what rapture
Will it fill Dean & Chapter!

42. Gay *to* Swift *22 October 1726*

Add. 4805

Dear Sir. / Before I say one word to you, give me leave to
say something of the other Gentleman's Affair.[1] The Letter
was sent, and the answer was, that every thing was finish'd,
& concluded according to orders; and that it would be
publickly known to be so in a very few days, so that I think
there can be no occasion for his writing any more about this
Affair.

The Letter you wrote to Mr Pope was not receiv'd 'till
eleven or twelve days after date, and the Post Office we

---

[1] The publication of *Gulliver's Travels*.

suppose have very vigilant Officers, for they had taken care
to make him pay for a double Letter. I wish I could tell you
that the cutting of the tendons of two of his fingers was a
joke, but it is really so. The wound is quite heald; his hand
is still weak, and the two fingers drop downwards as I told
you before, but I hope it will be very little troublesome or
detrimental to him.

In Answer to our Letter of Maps, Pictures & receipts,[1]
you call it a tripartite Letter; If you will examine it once
again, you will find some Lines of Mrs Howard, & some of
Mr Pulteney which you have not taken the least notice of.
The receipt of the Veal [is] of Monsieur Davaux Mr
Pulteney's Cook. and it hath been approv'd of at one of our
Twickenham entertainments. The difficulty of the Sauce-pan,
I believe you will find is owing to a negligence in perusing
the manuscript, for if I remember right it is there call'd a
Stew-pan. Your Earthen Vessell provided it is close stopt, I
allow to be a good succedaneum. As to the boiling Chickens
in a Wooden Bowle, I shall be quite asham'd to consult Mrs
Howard upon your account,[2] who thinks herself entirely
neglected by you in your not writing to her as you promis'd;
However Let her take it as she will, to serve a friend I will
venture to ask it of her; The Prince and his family come to
settle in town to morrow.[3] That Mr Pulteney expected an
answer to his Letter & would be extreamly pleas'd to hear
from you is very certain, for I have heard him talk of it with
expectation for above a fortnight. I have of late been very
much out of order with a slight feaver, which I am not yet
quite free from; it was occasion'd by a cold, which my
Attendance at the Guildhall improv'd. I have not a friend
who hath got any thing under my Administration but the
Dutchess of Queensberry who hath had a benefit of a thousand pounds. Your mentioning Mr Rollinson[4] so kindly will,
I know, give him much pleasure, for he always talks of you
with great regard and the strongest terms of friendship; He
hath of late been ill of a feaver, but is recover'd so as to go

---

[1] The 'Cheddar' letter.

[2] Swift had asked for Mrs. Howard's
recipe for 'Chicken in a wooden Boul'.
See Swift to Pope and Gay, 15 October
1726, *Swift Corr.* iii. 173.

[3] From Richmond.

[4] William Rollinson, a retired London wine merchant, friend of Swift,
Pope, Gay, and Bolingbroke.

abroad to take the Air. If the Gravers keep their word with me, I shall be able to publish my Fables soon after Christmas. The Doctor's book is entirely printed off, & will be very soon publish'd.[1] I believe you will expect that I should give you some account how I have spent my time since you left me. I have attended my distrest friend at Twickenham, & been his Emanuensis, which you know is no idle Charge, & I have read about half Virgil, & half Spenser's Fairy Queen.[2] I still despise Court Performents so that I lose no time upon attendance on great men, and still can find amusement enough without Quadrille, which here is the Universal Employment of Life. I thought you would be glad to hear from me, so that I determin'd not to stir out of my lodgings till I had answer'd your Letter, and I think I shall very probably hear more of the matter which I mention in the first paragraph of this Letter as soon as I go abroad, for I expect it every day. We have no news as yet of Mr Stopfort,[3] Mr Rollinson told me he shall know of his arrival, & will send me word. Lord Bolingbroke hath been to make a visit to Sir William Wyndham; I hear he is return'd, but I have not seen him. If I had been in a better State of health, & Mrs Howard were not to come to town to morrow, I would have gone to Mr Pope's to day to have din'd with him there on Monday. You ask me how to address to Lord B when you are dispos'd to write to him. If you mean Lord Burlington, he is not yet return'd from France, but is expected every day. If you mean Lord Bathurst he is in Gloucestershire & makes but a very short stay;[4] so that if you direct to one of them in St James's Square, or to the other at Burlington house in Piccadilly your Letter will find them. I will make your Compliments to Lord Chesterfield & Mr Pulteney, and I beg you in return to make mine to Mr Ford. Next Week I shall have a new coat & new Buttons for the Birth-day, though I dont know but a

[1] *Tables of Ancient Coins, Weights, and Measures* (1727).

[2] This is characteristic of many of Gay's letters to Swift, which so often adopt the tone of an undergraduate writing home.

[3] The Revd. James Stopford, close friend of Swift's, executor of his will and later Bishop of Cloyne. Swift had introduced Stopford to Gay and Pope by letter the year before. See Swift to Pope, 19 July 1725, *Swift Corr.* iii. 78.

[4] Swift means Bolingbroke, as Gay very well knows. See the postscript to this letter.

turncoat might have been more for my advantage. / Yours most sincerely & affectionately.

Whitehall. Octr. 22. 1726.

I hear that Lord Bolingbroke will be in town / at his house in Pell-mell next week.

Address: To / The Reverend Dr Swift / Dean of St Patrick's in / Dublin. / Ireland.
Endorsement: Mr Gay. Oct. 22d. 1726 [Swift's hand]

43. Gay *to* Swift *17 November 1726*

1740 (*Letters of Pope and Swift*)

Nov. 17. 1726.

About ten days ago a Book was publish'd here of the Travels of one Gulliver, which hath been the conversation of the whole town ever since: The whole impression sold in a week; and nothing is more diverting than to hear the different opinions people give of it, though all agree in liking it extreamly. 'Tis generally said that you are the Author, but I am told, the Bookseller declares he knows not from what hand it came. From the highest to the lowest it is universally read, from the Cabinet-council to the Nursery. The Politicians to a man agree, that it is free from particular reflections, but that the Satire on general societies of men is too severe. Not but we now and then meet with people of greater perspicuity, who are in search for particular applications in every leaf; and 'tis highly probable we shall have keys publish'd to give light into Gulliver's design. Your Lord ——[1] is the person who least approves it, blaming it as a design of evil consequence to depreciate human nature, at which it cannot be wondered that he takes most offence, being himself the most accomplish'd of his species, and so losing more than any other of that praise which is due both to the dignity and virtue of a man. Your friend, my Lord Harcourt, commends it very much, though he thinks in some places the matter too far carried. The Duchess Dowager of Marlborough is in

[1] Bolingbroke.

raptures at it; she says she can dream of nothing else since she read it: she declares, that she hath now found out, that her whole life hath been lost in caressing the worst part of mankind, and treating the best as her foes; and that if she knew Gulliver, tho' he had been the worst enemy she ever had, she would give up all her present acquaintance for his friendship. You may see by this, that you are not much injur'd by being suppos'd the Author of this piece. If you are, you have disoblig'd us, and two or three of your best friends, in not giving us the least hint of it while you were with us;[1] and in particular Dr. Arbuthnot, who says it is ten thousand pitys he had not known it, he could have added such abundance of things upon every subject. Among Lady-critics, some have found out that Mr. Gulliver had a particular malice to maids of honour. Those of them who frequent the Church, say, his design is impious, and that it is an insult on Providence, by depreciating the works of the Creator. Notwithstanding I am told the Princess hath read it with great pleasure. As to other Critics, they think the flying island is the least entertaining; and so great an opinion the town have of the impossibility of Gulliver's writing at all below himself, that 'tis agreed that Part was not writ by the same Hand, tho' this hath its defenders too. It hath pass'd Lords and Commons, *nemine contradicente*; and the whole town, men, women, and children are quite full of it.

Perhaps I may all this time be talking to you of a Book you have never seen, and which hath not yet reach'd Ireland; if it hath not, I believe what we have said will be sufficient to recommend it to your reading, and that you order me to send it to you.

But it will be much better to come over your self, and read it here, where you will have the pleasure of variety of commentators, to explain the difficult passages to you.

We all rejoyce that you have fixt the precise time of your coming to be *cum hirundine prima*; which we modern naturalists pronounce, ought to be reckon'd, contrary to Pliny in

[1] Perhaps this is an effort on Gay's part to deceive the postal authorities who occasionally opened and read suspect anti-government mail. See Letter 79; see also Chesterfield to Mrs. Howard [August 1733], *Suffolk Corr.* ii. 62. Or perhaps Gay is simply playing Swift's game of the mysterious origin of *Gulliver* to the hilt.

this northern latitude of fifty-two degrees, from the end of February, Styl Greg. at farthest. But to us your friends, the coming of such a black swallow as you, will make a summer in the worst of seasons. We are no less glad at your mention of Twickenham and Dawley; and in town you know you have a lodging at Court.[1]

The Princess is cloath'd in Irish silk; pray give our service to the Weavers. We are strangely surpriz'd to hear that the Bells in Ireland ring without your money;[2] I hope you do not write the thing that is not. We are afraid that B——[3] hath been guilty of that crime, that you (like a Houyhnhnm) have treated him as a Yahoo, and discarded him your service. I fear you do not understand these modish terms, which every creature now understands but your self.

You tell us your Wine is bad, and that the Clergy do not frequent your house, which we look upon to be tautology. The best advice we can give you is, to make them a present of your wine, and come away to better.

You fancy we envy you, but you are mistaken, we envy those you are with, for we cannot envy the man we love. Adieu.

44. Gay *to* Brigadier James Dormer *22 November 1726*

Rousham MSS.

Dear Sir. / Though you have heard from me but once in form,[4] it hath not been either for want of respect or friendship. I had the pleasure to hear of your health by the return of the fleet, and I really would have writ to you often, if I did not look upon myself as an unnecessary correspondence. I have as little prospect of being provided for as ever, so that I have not had the least good fortune to make me some amends for the loss of your company. I am about to publish

---

[1] Gay's apartment at Whitehall.

[2] As a result of the *Drapier's Letters*, Swift was extremely popular in Ireland at this time. On his return to Dublin in August 1726 he was given a hero's welcome, which included ringing the bells of St. Patrick's. See Mist's *Weekly Journal*, 3 September 1726.

[3] Probably a misprint for 'P', meaning Proudfoot, Swift's agent, as Ball suggested.

[4] 30 October 1725.

a collection of Fables entirely of my own invention to be dedicated to Prince William, they consist of fifty, and I am oblig'd to Mr Kent & Wootton[1] for the Designs of the Plates. The Work is begun to be printed, and is delay'd only upon account of the Gravers, who are neither very good or expeditious. I believe you must have heard that Mr Pelham is married to Lady Katharine Manners. Tis said that Mr Arundell is married to Lady Fanny, but as he is in the country, I believe, 'tis only the conjecture of the town. We have a Book lately publish'd here which hath of late taken up the whole conversation of the town. Tis said to be writ by Swift. It is called, The travells of Lemuell Gulliver in two Volumes. It hath had a very great sale. People differ vastly in their opinions of it, for some think it hath a great deal of wit, but others say, it hath none at all. As it hath been publish'd about a month, I fancy you must have either heard of it or seen it. We have a famous French Author in town, who upon a Quarrell with the Chevalier de Rohan is banish'd his Country. He hath been here about half a year, and begins to speak English very well. His name is Voltaire, the Author of Oedipe. He hath finish'd his Poem of the Ligue,[2] which he intends to publish in England in Quarto with very fine copper plates which he hath got already grav'd by the best Gravers in Paris. I am told the Parliament will not sit till about the middle of January, so that the town is yet but thin. There is a set of Italian Comedians who act twice a week at the Opera house, but they are very little approv'd off, for the Harlequin is very indifferent, so that they find but small encouragement. I was at Rousham twice last summer in a visit which I find extreamly improv'd,[3] and your Brother was with us once or twice at Middleton. Lord and Lady Burlington are return'd from Paris where they made a stay of about two months. Lord Chesterfield designs to take Lord Cadogan's house in case the Duke of Richmond does not go into

---

[1] John Wootton (1668?–1765), animal and landscape painter. See *DNB* entry.

[2] *La Ligue ou Henri le Grand*, published in March 1728 by Woodman & Lyons, Russell Street. See Archibald Ballantyne, *Voltaire's Visit to England, 1726–1729* (1919), pp. 149–51.

[3] Kent had done some work at Rousham, renovating the library and landscaping the grounds. See Horace Walpole, *Correspondence with George Montague*, Yale Edition, IX. i (1941), p. 290; see also *Earls*, p. 145.

it himself, in which as yet he is undetermin'd. All the Goods of my Lord Cadogan are to [be] dispos'd off by auction in the month of January next. You see, I send you the little trifling news of the town, I leave that of more consequence to others. I long for your company, but since I cannot have it, I wish I could be serviceable to you in any thing you will please to command me. / Dear Sir, / I am / Your most obedient and / most faithfull Servant / J Gay.

Whitehall, near the Chappell.

Novemr. 22. 1726.

Address: A Son Excellence / Mr Dormer Envoyé Extraordinaire / de sa Majesté Britannique / a Lisbonne / Portugal.

Endorsement: Mr. Gay / Novr. 22 os. 1726 [Presumably Dormer's hand]

45. Gay *to* Swift *18 February 1726/7*

Add. 4805

Dear Sir. / I believe tis now my turn to write to you, though Mr Pope hath taken all I have to say & put it in a long Letter, which is sent too by Mr Stopfort,[1] but however I could not omit this occasion of thanking you for his acquaintance; I don't know whether I ought to thank you or no, considering I have lost him so soon; though he hath given me some hopes of seeing him again in the summer. He will give you an account of our negotiations together, and I may now glory in my success, since I could contribute to his.[2] We din'd together to day at the Doctor's, who with me was in high delight upon an information Mr Stopfort gave us, that we are like to see you soon. My Fables are printed, but I cannot get my plates finish'd, which hinders the publication. I expect nothing, & am like to get nothing. tis needless to write for Mr Stopfort can acquaint you of my Affairs more fully than I can in a letter. Mrs Howard desires me to make her Compliments, she hath been in an ill state (as to her

---

[1] In addition to Gay's letter, Stopford, on his way back to Ireland from the Continent, carried letters from Pope and Bolingbroke.

[2] Stopford's social 'success' while in London.

64

health) all this winter, but I hope is somewhat better. I have
been very much out of order myself for the most part of the
winter, upon my being let blood last week, my Cough & my
head ach are better. Mrs Blount always asks after you. I
refus'd supping at Burlington house to night in regard to my
health, & this morning I walk'd two hours in the Park.
Bow'rey[1] told me this morning Mr Pope had a Cold, but
that Mrs Pope is pretty well. The contempt of the world
grows upon me, and I now begin to be richer and richer, for
I find I could every morning I wake be content with less than
I aim'd at the day before. I fancy in time, I shall bring myself
into that state which No man ever knew before me, in thinking I have enough. I really am afraid to be content with so
little, Lest my good friends should censure me for indolence,
and the want of laudable ambition, so that it will be absolutely necessary for me to improve my fortune to content
them. How solicitous is mankind to please others!

Pray, give my sincere service to Mr Ford. Dear Sir /
Yours most Affectionately. / JG.

Whitehall. Feb. 18th. 1726/7.

Address: To / Dr Swift / Dean of St Patrick's. / Dublin.
Endorsement: Mr Gay / Feb. 18–1726–7 [Swift's hand]

46. Gay *to* Pope[2] [*October 1727*]

1745 (Ayre, *Memoirs of Pope*)

Dear Mr. Pope, / My Melancholy increases, and every Hour
threatens me with some Return of my Distemper; nay, I

---

[1] Pope's waterman.

[2] Following Ayre's lead (*Memoirs of Pope*, ii. 118), Sherburn dated this letter March 1728/9 on the assumption that Gay's tirade against the Court was prompted by the *Polly* débâcle and especially by the Duchess of Queens-berry's banishment from Court, which occurred on 1 March 1728/9. See *Pope Corr*. iii. 19, n. 3. There are two basic objections to this dating.

In the first place, Ayre confuses cause and effect rather curiously. He writes (p. 118): 'When all his [Gay's] Expecta-tions from the Court were thus reduced to nothing, Mr. Pope, before this last Letter, wrote him one in a Boldness of Spirit, and with Freedom; fit to be seen and read by him, but never meant to be the Object of the public Eye.' Pope called his letter of 16 October 1727 a 'congratulatory letter' on Gay's being think I may rather say I have it on me. Not the divine Looks, the kind Favours and Expressions of the divine Dutchess, who hereafter shall be in Place of a Queen to me, (nay, she shall be my Queen) nor the inexpressible Goodness of the Duke, can in the least chear me. The Drawing-Room no more receives Light from those two Stars. There is now what *Milton* says is in Hell, Darkness visible.[1]—O that I had never known what a Court was! Dear *Pope*, what a barren Soil (to me so) have I been striving to produce something out of! Why did I not take your Advice before my writing Fables for the Duke, not to write them? Or rather, to write them for some young Nobleman? It is my very hard Fate, I must get nothing, write for them or against them. I find myself in such a strange Confusion and Depression of Spirits, that I have not Strength even to make my Will; though I perceive, by many Warnings, I have no continuing City here.[2] I begin to look upon myself as one already dead; and desire, my dear Mr. *Pope*, (whom I love as my own Soul) if you survive me, (as you certainly will) that you will, if a Stone should mark the Place of my Grave, see these Words put on it:

free from the Court, and it was an obvious attempt by Pope to cheer up a despondent Gay. Yet, Ayre dates Pope's letter *prior* to Gay's letter (above) telling Pope of his despondency. The 'congratulatory letter' was clearly a reply to Gay's melancholy missive printed above, and this argues for dating Gay's letter sometime prior to 16 October 1727, the date of Pope's reply. Moreover, with a 1728/9 dating, the 'Expectations from the Court', of which Ayre speaks, are puzzling. By the time of writing *Polly* Gay had come to recognize that his long quest for a place had ended in failure. On 20 March 1727/8, for example, he wrote to Swift that he was leaving London for Bath, 'for I have no expectations of receiving any favours from the Court'. In October 1727, however, his expectations had been high and they had, indeed, been 'reduced to nothing' by the announcement of his appointment to the menial post of Gentleman-Usher

to the two-year-old Princess Louisa. On the strength of his dedication of the *Fables* to Prince William, Gay had expected much more from the Queen and he was bitterly disappointed. The letter (above) is thoroughly consistent with his state of mind at this time.

Secondly, if the March 1728/9 dating be accepted, it is difficult to reconcile Gay's abject despair in this letter with the elation he displays elsewhere at the time over *Polly*'s success in its published form, and with the gratification he evinces at the favour accorded him by friends who championed his cause. See, for instance, Letter 55.

The October 1727 dating is reinforced by Gay's reference to his 'distemper'. He had been seriously ill during the winter and spring of 1727. See Letter 45; see also Congreve to Pope, 6 May [1727], *Pope Corr.* ii. 433.

[1] *Paradise Lost*, i. 63.
[2] Heb. xiii. 14.

> Life is a Jest, and all Things show it;
> I thought so once, but now I know it.

With what more you may think proper.

If any Body should ask, how I could communicate this after Death? Let it be known, it is not meant so, but my present Sentiment in Life. What the Bearer brings besides this Letter, should I die without a Will, (which I am the likelier to do, as the Law will settle my small Estate much as I should myself) let it remain with you, as it has long done with me, a Remembrance of a dead Friend:[1] But there is none like you, living or dead.

I am, dear Mr. Pope, | Your's, &c. JOHN GAY.

47. Gay *and* Pope *to* Swift *22 October 1727*

1740 (*Letters of Pope and Swift*)

Oct. 22, 1727

Though you went away from us so unexpectedly, and in so clandestine a manner; yet by several enquiries, we have inform'd our selves of every thing that hath happen'd to you.

To our great joy you have told us your deafness left you at the Inn in Aldersgate-street:[2] No doubt your ears knew there was nothing worth hearing in England.

Our advices from Chester tell us, that you met Captain Lawson; the Captain was a man of veracity, and set sail at the time he told you; I really wish'd you had laid hold of that opportunity, for you had then been in Ireland the next day:[3] Besides, as it is credibly reported, the Captain had a bottle or two of excellent claret in his Cabbin. You would not then have had the plague of that little smoaky room at Holy-head; but considering it was there you lost your giddiness, we have great reason to praise smoaky rooms for the future, and prescribe them in like cases to our friends. The maid of the

---

[1] The keepsake is unidentified.

[2] In a letter to Pope, 12 October 1727, *Swift Corr.* iii. 242. The coach for Chester left from Aldersgate Street.

[3] Swift, impatient at a slight delay in the departure of the government yacht, captained by Lawson, from Parkgate (12 miles NW. of Chester) to Dublin, went on to Holyhead, where he was held up for over a week by adverse winds. See Swift's 'Holyhead Journal', *Prose Works*, ed. Temple Scott, xi. 391–403.

house writes us word,[1] that while you were there you were busy for ten days together writing continually—and that as Wat drew nearer and nearer to Ireland, he blunder'd more and more. By a scrap of paper left in this smoaky room, it seem'd as if the Book you was writing, was a most lamentable account of your travels; and really, had there been any wine in the house, the place would not have been so irksome. We were further told, that you set out, was driven back again by a storm, and lay in the ship all night. After the next setting sail, we were in great concern about you, because the weather grew very tempestuous. When to my great joy, and surprize, I receiv'd a letter from Carlingford in Ireland, which inform'd us that after many perils you were safely landed there. Had the oysters been good it would have been a comfortable refreshment after your fatigue. We compassionated you in your travels through that country of desolation and poverty in your way to Dublin, for it is a most dreadful circumstance to have lazy dull horses on a road where there is very bad or no Inns. When you carry a sample of English Apples next to Ireland, I beg you would either get them from Gutheridge or Devonshire.[2] Pray who was the Clergyman that met you at some distance from Dublin? because we could not learn his name.[3] These are all the hints we could get of your long and dangerous journey, every step of which we shar'd your anxieties—and all that we have now left to comfort us, is to hear that you are in good health.

But why should we tell you what you know already? The Queen's family is at last settled, and in the list I was appointed Gentleman-usher to the Princess Louisa, the youngest Princess; which, upon account that I am so far advanc'd in life, I have declin'd accepting; and have endeavour'd, in the best manner I could, to make my excuses by a letter to her Majesty. So now all my expectations are vanish'd; and I have no prospect, but in depending wholly upon my self, and my own conduct. As I am us'd to disappointments I can bear them, but as I can have no more hopes, I can no more be

---

[1] The details of Swift's ordeal at Holyhead actually reached Gay and Pope in a letter from Swift's close friend, the Revd. Thomas Sheridan.

[2] Swift's ancestors were from Goodrich (Gutheridge) in Herefordshire and Gay was born in Barnstaple, Devonshire. [3] Probably Sheridan.

disappointed, so that I am in a blessed condition.—You remember you were advising me to go into Newgate to finish my scenes the more correctly—I now think I shall, for I have no attendance to hinder me; but my Opera is already finished.[1] I leave the rest of this paper to Mr. Pope.

Gay is a free-man, and I writ him a long congratulatory letter upon it. Do you the same: It will mend him, and make him a better man than a Court could do. Horace might keep his coach in Augustus's time, if he pleas'd, but I won't in the time of our Augustus. My Poem[2] (which it grieves me that I dare not send you a copy of, for fear of the Curl's and Dennis's of Ireland, and still more for fear of the worst of Traytors, our friends and Admirers) my Poem, I say, will shew you what a distinguishing age we lived in? Your name is in it, with some others under a mark of such ignominy as you will not much grieve to wear in that company. Adieu, and God bless you, and give you health and spirits.

> *Whether you chuse Cervantes' serious air,*
> *Or laugh and shake in Rablais' easy chair,*
> *Or in the graver Gown instruct mankind,*
> *Or silent, let thy morals tell thy mind.*

These two verses are over and above what I've said of you in the Poem. Adieu.

48. Gay *to* Edward Harley, Earl of Oxford[3]
[*12 February 1727/8*]

Longleat Portland MSS.

My Lord / I was last night to pay my duty to your Lordship, and to thank you for interesting yourself in so kind a manner in my behalf. I had heard before, that the King & Queen were to be present at Julius Caesar on Friday, so that

---

[1] *The Beggar's Opera.*
[2] *The Dunciad.*
[3] The dating is based on Oxford's endorsement and the fact that 12 February 1727/8 fell on a Monday. According to the account book of the Theatre Royal for the 1727-8 season, now in the Houghton Library, Harvard, two tickets were reserved in Gay's name on 19 February and picked up by Lady Oxford's servant on 26 February.

my intention was to acquaint your Lordship that I had fixt on Thursday. As to the Boxes on that day, I fear by what I have heard about the town, they are taken up already, but if your Lordship would be so good as to send a servant to the Boxkeeper, I hope I shall have the honour of Lady Oxford's presence in the very Box she chuses, for I know Mr Rich would upon all occasions be very glad to oblige your Lordship / I am / My Lord / your Lordship's / Most obedient & / Most oblig'd humble / Servant / J Gay

Whitehall / Monday morning.

Endorsement: Mr Gay / Whitehall Feb: 12: 1727/8 [Presumably Oxford's hand]

49. Gay *to* Swift *15 February 1727/8*

Add. 4805

Dear Sir / I have deferr'd writing to you from time to time till I could give you an account of the Beggar's Opera. It is Acted at the Playhouse in Lincoln's Inn fields, with such success that the Playhouse hath been crouded every night; to night is the fifteenth time of Acting, and 'tis thought it will run a fortnight longer.[1] I have order'd Motte to send the Play to you the first opportunity. I made no interest either for approbation or money nor hath any body been prest to take tickets for my Benefit, notwithstanding which, I think I shall make an addition to my fortune of between six and seven hundred pounds. I know this account will give you pleasure, as I have push'd through this precarious Affair without servility or flattery. As to any favours from Great men I am in the same state you left me; but I am a great deal happier as I have no expectations. The Dutchess of Queensberry hath signaliz'd her friendship to me upon this occasion in such a conspicuous manner, that I hope (for her sake) you will take care to put your fork to all its proper uses, and suffer nobody for the f[uture] to put their knives in their

---

[1] *The Beggar's Opera* ultimately ran a total of sixty-two nights, a record for that time. See W. E. Schultz, *Gay's Beggar's Opera* (1923), pp. 7–10.

mouths.[1] Lord Cobham says that I should [have] printed it in Italian over against the English, that the Ladys might have understood what they read. The outlandish (as they now call it) Opera hath been so thin of late that some have call'd that the Beggars Opera, & if the run continues, I fear I shall have remonstrances drawn up against me by the Royal Academy of Musick.[2] As none of us have heard from you of late every one of us are in concern about your health. I beg we may hear from you soon. By my constant attendance on this affair I have almost worried myself into an ill state of health, but I intend in five or six days to go to our Country seat at Twickenham for a little air. Mr Pope is very seldom in town. Mrs Howard frequently asks after you, & desires her compliments to you; Mr George Arbuthnot, the Doctor's Brother is married to Mrs Peggy Robinson. I would write more, but as to night is for my Benefit, I am in a hurry to go out about business. / I am Dear Sir / Your most affectionate / & obedient Servant / J Gay.

Whitehall. / Febr. 15. 1727/8 / My Service to Dr Delany

Address: To / The Reverend Dr Swift / Dean of St Patricks in / Dublin / Ireland.
Postmark: 15/FE
Endorsements: [In Swift's hand] Mr Gay. / Feb. 22d. 1727–8
                          Ansd. May. 11th. 1728.

50. Gay *to* Swift *20 March 1727/8*

Add. 4805

Dear Sir. / I am extreamly sorry that your disorder is return'd, but as you have a medicine which hath twice remov'd [it?] you, I hope by this time, have again found the good effects of it. I have seen Dr Delany at my Lodgings, but as I have been for a few days with Mr Pulteney at

---

[1] During his stay at Twickenham in the summer of 1727 Swift was observed using his knife to convey food to his mouth and was teased about his questionable table manners. Swift blamed it all on Pope's two-pronged forks or, as he called them, 'poetical forks'. See Swift to Gay, 10 November 1730, *Swift Corr*. iii. 417.

[2] Which sponsored the Italian Opera.

Cashioberry[1] I have not yet return'd his visit, I went with him to wait upon Lord Bathurst & Lord Bolingbroke both of whom desire me to make you their compliments. Lady Boling-broke was very much out of order, and with my Lord is now at Doyley;[2] she expects a letter from you. Mrs Howard would gladly have the receipt you have found so much benefit by; she is happier than I have seen her ever since you left us, for she is free as to her conjugal affairs by articles of agreement.[3] The Beggar's Opera hath now been acted thirty six times, and was as full the last night as the first, and as yet there is not the least probability of a thin audience; though there is a discourse about the town that the Directors of the Royal Academy of Musick design to sollicite against it's being play'd on the *outlandish* Opera days, as it is now call'd. On the Benefit day of one of the Actresse's last week one of the players falling sick they were oblig'd to give out another play or dismiss the Audience, A Play was given out, but the people call'd out for the Beggar's Opera, & they were forc'd to play it, or the Audience would not have stayd. I have got by all this success between seven & eight hundred pounds, and Rich, (deducting the whole charges of the House) hath clear'd already near four thousand pounds.[4] In about a month I am going to the Bath with the Dutchess of Marl-borough and Mr Congreve, for I have no expectations of receiving any favours from the Court. The Dutchess of Queensberry is in Wiltshire, where she hath had the small pox in so favourable a way, that she had not above seven or eight in her face; she is now perfectly recover'd. There is a Mezzo-tinto Print publish'd to day of Polly, the Heroine of the Beggar's Opera,[5] who was before unknown, & is now

---

[1] Cashiobury or Cassiobury Park, near Watford, Hertfordshire, estate of Gay's quondam hunting companion, the Earl of Essex. See Letter 4.

[2] Dawley.

[3] The Howards' marital dispute, a *cause célèbre* at Court during the winter of 1727/8, was settled on the basis of the King's agreeing to pay the 'injured' husband, Charles Howard, £1,200 a year. See *Lord Hervey's Memoirs*, ed. Romney Sedgwick (1963), pp. 17–18, 87–89; see also Gay's 'Memorandum' (Appendix).

[4] Which establishes the traditional *bon mot* that *The Beggar's Opera* made 'Gay rich and Rich gay' as more poetry than truth.

[5] The mezzotint of Polly was by John Faber the Younger (1695 ?–1756), after a painting by John 'Jack' Ellys or Ellis (1701–57). Ellys, a student of Thorn-hill's, and later co-director, with Hogarth, of the Academy in St. Martin's Lane, also painted Thomas Walker as Macheath (see Letter 51), which Faber engraved. The whereabouts of Ellys's

in so high vogue, that I am in doubt, whether her fame does not surpass that of the Opera itself.[1] I would not have talk'd so much upon this subject, or upon any thing that regards myself but to you; but as I know you interest yourself so sincerely in every thing that concerns me, I believe you would have blam'd me if I had said less. Your Singer owes Dr Arbuthnot some money, I have forgot the sum; I think it is two Guineas; the Dr desir'd me to let you know it.[2] I saw him last night with Mr Lewis at Sir William Wyndham's, who if he had not the Gout would have answer'd your Letter you sent him a year & a half ago; he said this to me a week since, but he is now pretty well again, & so may forget to write, for which reason, I ought to do him justice and tell you that I think him a sincere well wisher of yours. I have not seen Mr Pope lately, but have heard that both he & Mrs Pope are very well. I intend to see him at Twickenham on sunday next. I have not drunk out the Gutheridge Cyder yet, but I have not so much as a single pint of Port in my Cellar. I have bought two pair of Sheets against your coming to town, so that we need not send any more to Jervas upon that ac[count.] I really miss you every day, and I would be content th[at] yo[u shoul]d have one whole window to yourself, & half [another] to have you again. I am / Dear Sir / Yours most affectionately.

You have a half years interest due / at Lady-day, & now 'tis March. 20th. 1727/8.

Address: To / The Reverend Dr Swift / Dean of St Patrick's in / Dublin / Ireland
Postmark: 21/MR
Endorsement: [In Swift's hand] Mr Gay. Mar. 20. 1727–8
Answd. Mar. 28th

paintings is unknown but copies of Faber's engravings may be seen in the Print Room, The British Museum, or in the National Portrait Gallery.
   [1] For the rewards which Lavinia Fenton's fame as Polly brought her, see Letter 52 and footnote.
   [2] See also Letter 40 and Swift to Gay, 28 March 1728, *Swift Corr.* iii. 277.

51. Gay *to* Swift *16 May 1728*

Add. 4805

Dear Sir / I have been at the Bath about ten days, and I have play'd at no Game but once and that at Back-Gammon with Mr Lewis who is very much your humble Servant. He is here upon account of the ill-state of health of his Wife who hath as yet found very little benefit by the waters. Lord & Lady Bolingbroke are here, I think she is better than when I came here, they stay, as I guess, only about a fortnight longer; they both desird me to make their compliments, as does Mr Congreve, who is in a very ill state of health, but somewhat better since he came here. Mr Lewis tells me that he is promis'd to receive a hundred pounds upon your account at his return to London;[1] he having (upon request) comply'd to stay for the payment 'till that time. The two hundred pounds you left with me are in the hands of Lord Bathurst together with some money of mine, all which he will repay at Midsummer, so that we must think of some other way of employing it, and I cannot resolve what to do.

I dont know how long I shall stay here, because I am now, as I have been all my life at the disposal of others. I drink the waters, and am in hopes to lay in a stock of health, some of which I wish to communicate to you. Dr Delany told me you had been upon a journey, and I really fancy taking horse is as good as taking the waters. I hope you have found benefit by it. The Beggar's Opera is acted here, but our Polly here hath got no fame, but the Actor's have got money. I have sent by Dr Delany the Opera Polly Peachum, & Captain Macheath,[2] I would have sent you my own head which is now graving to make up the Gang, but it is not yet finish'd.[3]

---

[1] Probably part of the payment Swift received for *Gulliver's Travels*.

[2] i.e. a copy of the play together with mezzotints of Lavinia Fenton (Polly) and Thomas Walker (Macheath).

[3] The mezzotint engraving of Gay was by Francis Kyte after a portrait by William Aikman (1682–1731), which had been commissioned by Mrs.

Howard. See also Letter 52, where Gay speaks of the mezzotint as being 'publish'd'.

There is an Aikman portrait of Gay in the Scottish National Portrait Gallery, Edinburgh, but this appears to be an earlier painting. The whereabouts of 'Mrs. Howard's painting' is unknown.

I suppose you must have heard that I have had the honour to have had a Sermon preach'd against my works by a Court Chaplain, which I look upon as no small addition to my fame.[1] direct to me here when you write, and the sooner that is, the sooner you will make me happy.

Bath. May. 16 1728.

Address: To / The Revd Dr Swift Dean of St / Patrick's in / Dublin. / Ireland.

Endorsement: Mr Gay / May. 16th. 1728 [Swift's hand]

52. Gay *to* Swift 6 *July* 1728

Add. 4805

Dear Sir. / The last news I heard of you was from Mr Lancelot who was at this place with Lord Sussex, who gave me hope of seeing of you the latter end of this summer; I wish you may keep that resolution, & take the Bathe in your way to town. You in all probability will find here some or most of those you like to see. Dr Arbuthnot writ to me to day from Tunbridge where he is now for the recovery of his health, having had several relapses of a feaver, he tells me, that he is much better since he came there, & that in August he intends to come hither. Mr Lewis will be here the beginning of August, & I have some hopes of seeing Mr Pope too. Mr Congreve & I often talk of you, & wish you health & every good thing, but often out of self interest we wish you with us. In five or six days I set out upon an excursion to Herefordshire to Lady Scudamore's, but shall return here in the beginning of August. I wish you could meet me at Gutheridge. The Bathe did not agree with Lady Bolingbroke, & she went from hence much worse than she came; since she came to Dawley, by her own inclination without the advice of Physicians, she hath taken to a Milk diet, & she hath writ me an account of prodigious good effects both

---

[1] In March Dr. Thomas Herring, then King's Chaplain and later Archbishop of York and of Canterbury, delivered a sermon in Lincoln's Inn Chapel condemning *The Beggar's Opera* for presenting crime in a favourable light. See Schultz, *Gay's Beggar's Opera*, pp. 226–8; see also Swift's 'A Vindication of Mr. Gay and *The Beggar's Opera*'.

of recovery of her appetite & Spirits. The weather is extreamly hot, the place is very empty, I have an inclination to Study but the heat makes it impossible. The D[uke] of Bolton I hear hath run away with Polly Peachum, having settled 400ł a year upon her during pleasure, & upon dis- agreement 200ł a year.[1] Mr Pope is in a State of Persecution for the Dunciad, I wish to be witness of his fortitude, but he writes but seldom. 'Twould be a consolation to me to hear from you, I have heard but once from Mrs Howard these 3 months, & I think but once from Mr Pope. My Portrait Metzotinto is publish'd from Mrs Howard's painting, I wish I could contrive to send you one, but I fancy I could get a better impression at London. I have ten thousand things to talk to you but few to write, but deferr writing to you no longer knowing you interest yourself in everything that con- cerns me so much that I make you happy, as you will me, if you can tell me you are in good health; Which I wish to hear every morning as soon as I wake./ I am Dear Sir Yours most affectionately.

Bathe. July. 6. 1728.

Address: To / The Reverend Dr Swift / Dean of St Patricks in / Dublin / Ireland.
Postmark: 8/ɪʏ
Endorsement: July. 6th. 1728 / Mr Gay [Swift's hand]

53. Gay *to* Pope *2 August 1728*

1737 (*Letters of Mr. Alexander Pope*)

Aug. 2, 1728

'Twas two or three weeks ago that I writ you a letter: I might indeed have done it sooner; I thought of you every post-day upon that account, and every other day upon some account or other. I must beg you to give Mrs. B.[2] my sincere thanks for her kind way of thinking of me, which I have heard of more than once from our friend at court,[3] who seem'd in the letter she writ to be in high health and spirits.

---

[1] On the death of his wife in 1751 the Duke made Polly (Lavinia Fenton) Duchess of Bolton.   [2] Mrs. Blount.   [3] Mrs. Howard.

Considering the multiplicity of the pleasures and delights
that one is over-run with in those places, I wonder how any
body hath health and spirits enough to support 'em: I am
heartily glad she has, and whenever I hear so, I find it con-
tributes to mine. You see I am not free from dependance,
tho' I have less attendance than I had formerly; for a great
deal of my own welfare still depends upon hers. Is the widow's
house to be dispos'd of yet?[1] I have not given up my pretensions to the Dean; if it was to be parted with, I wish one of
us had it: I hope you wish so too, and that Mrs. Blount and
Mrs. Howard wish the same, and for the very same reason
that I wish it. All I could hear of you of late hath been by
advertisements in news-papers, by which one wou'd think
the race of Curls was multiplied; and by the indignation such
fellows show against you, that you have more merit than any
body alive could have. Homer himself hath not been worse
us'd by the French. I am to tell you that the Duchess[2] makes
you her compliments, and is always inclin'd to like any thing
you do; that Mr. Congreve admires, with me, your fortitude;
and loves, not envys your performance, for we are not
Dunces. Adieu.

54. Gay *to* Swift *2 December 1728*

Add. 4805

London Decemr. 2. 1728.

Dear Sir. / I think this is my 4th Letter, I am sure tis the
third without any answer. If I had had any assurance of your
health I should have been more easy. I should have writ to
you upon this subject above a month ago had it not been for
a report that you were upon the road in your way to England,
which I fear now was without any foundation. Your money
with part of my own is still in the hands of Lord Bathurst
which I believe he will keep no longer, but repay upon his

[1] Evidently a house by the Thames
where Gay might be near Pope and
Mrs. Howard. See *Pope Corr.* ii. 508,
n. 2. It was most likely the property of
the Widow Vernon, Thomas Vernon of
Twickenham having died in 1726 (see
Cobbett, *Memorials of Twickenham*,
p. 66). On the 'widow's house' see also
Letters 60 and 61.

[2] Gay was writing from Bath, where,
with the exception of the 'excursion to
Herefordshire' (Letter 52), he had been
since early May with Congreve and
Henrietta, Duchess of Marlborough.

coming to town; when I will endeavour to dispose of it as I do of my own unless I receive your orders to the contrary. Lord and Lady Bolingbroke are in town, she hath lately been very ill, but is now somewhat better. I have had a very severe attack of a feaver which by the care of our friend Dr Arbuthnot hath I hope now almost left me; I have been confin'd about ten days but never to my bed, so that I hope soon to get abroad about my business, which is, the care of the second part of the Beggar's Opera[1] which was almost ready for rehearsal. But Rich receiv'd the Duke of Grafton's[2] commands (upon an information he was rehearsing a Play improper to be represented) not to rehearse any new Play whatever 'till his Grace hath seen it; what will become of it I know not, but I am sure I have written nothing that can be legally supprest, unless the setting vices in general in an odious light, and virtue in an amiable one may give offence. I past five or six months this year at the Bath with the Dutchess of Marlborough, and then, in the view of taking care of myself, writ this peice. If it goes on, in case of success, I have taken care to make better bargains for myself, I tell you this, because I know you are so good to interest yourself so warmly in my affairs, that 'tis what you would want to know. I saw Mr Pope on friday, who as to his health is just as you left him; his mother, by his account is much the same. Mr Lewis, who is very much your servant, (as are all I have mention'd) tells me further time is still desir'd of him about the 100ł.[3] Dr Arbuthnot particularly desires his compliments, & Mrs Howard often asks after you. Prince Frederic is expected over this week.[4] I hope to go abroad in two or 3 days; I wish I could meet you either abroad or at home.

Endorsement: Mr Gay. Decr. 2d. 1728 [Swift's hand]

55. Gay *to* Swift *18 March 1728/9*

Add. 4805

Dear Sir / I have writ to you several times, and having heard nothing from you makes me fear my Letters have

---

[1] *Polly.* [2] The Lord Chamberlain. [4] Frederick Louis, Prince of Wales,
[3] See Letter 51.   who had remained in Hanover.

miscarried;[1] Mr Pope's Letter hath taken off my concern
in some degree, but I hope good weather will entirely re-
establish you in your health. I am but just recover'd from the
severest fit of sickness that ever any body had who escap'd
death; I was several times given up by the Physicians and
every body that attended me; and upon my recovery was
judg'd to be in so ill a condition that I should be miserable
for the remainder of my life, but contrary to all expectation
I am perfectly recover'd, and have no remainders of the dis-
tempers that attack'd me, which were at the same time,
Feaver, Asthma & Pleuresie. I am now in the Duke of
Queensberry's house,[2] and have been so ever since I left
Hampstead, where I was carried at a time that it was thought
I could not live a day. Since my coming to town, I have been
very little abroad, the weather has been so severe: I must
acquaint you, (because I know 'twill please you) that during
my Sickness I had many of the kindest proofs of friendship,
particularly from the Duke & Dutchess of Queensberry,
who, if I had been their nearest relation and nearest friend
could not have treated me with more constant attendance
then, and they continue the same to me now.

You must undoubtedly have heard that the Dutchess took
up my defence with the King and Queen in the cause of my
Play, and that she hath been forbid the Court for interesting
herself to increase my fortune for the publication of it without being acted; the Duke too hath given up his employment
which he would have done, if the Dutchess had not met this
treatment, upon account of ill usage from the Ministers; but
this hasten'd him in what he had determin'd. The Play is now
almost printed with the Musick, words & Basses engrav'd on
31 Copper plates, which by my friends assistance hath a
probability to turn greatly to my advantage.[3] The Dutchess

[1] Unless some intervening letters have
been lost, Gay had not heard from Swift
for nearly a year (28 March 1728).
Arbuthnot also complained of Swift's
negligence in writing during this period.
See Arbuthnot to Swift, 19 March
1728/9, *Swift Corr.* iii. 325; Arbuthnot
to Swift, 8 May 1729, *Swift Corr.* iii.
332.
[2] On the north side of Burlington

Gardens, between Saville Row and Old
Burlington St. See Laurence Hutton,
Literary Landmarks of London (1885),
p. 112.
[3] *Polly* was published by Gay, at his
own expense, on 25 March 1729. The
lengthy list of subscriptions, at one
guinea each, headed by Henrietta, the
Duchess of Marlborough's subscription
of £100, ensured the success of the venture.

of Marlborough hath given me a hundred pound for one Copy, & others have contributed very handsomely but as my account is not yet settled I cannot tell you particulars.

For writing in the cause of Virtue and against the fashionable vices, I am look'd upon at present as the most obnoxious person almost in England, Mr Pulteney tells me I have got the start of him. Mr Pope tells me that I am dead and that this obnoxiousness is the reward for my inoffensiveness in my former life. I wish I had a Book ready to send you, but I believe I shall not be able to compleat the work 'till the latter end of next week. Your Money is still in Lord Bathurst's hands, but I believe I shall receive it soon; I wish to receive your orders how to dispose of it. I am impatient to finish my work, for I want the country air, not that I am ill, but to recover my strength, and I cannot leave my work till it is finish'd. While I am writing this, I am [in] the room next to our dining room with sheets all-round it, and two people from the Binder folding sheets. I print the Book at my own expence in Quarto, which is to be sold for six shillings with the Musick. You see I dont want industry, and I hope you will allow that I have not the worst Oeconomy. Mrs Howard hath declar'd herself strongly both to the King & Queen as my advocate. The Dutchess of Queensberry is allow'd to have shown, more Spirit, more honour, and more goodness than was thought possible in our times; I should have added too more understanding and good sense. You see my fortune (as I hope my Virtue will) increases by oppression. I go to no courts, I drink no wine, and am calumniated even by Ministers of State, and yet am in good Spirits. Most of the Courtiers, though otherways my friends, refuse to contribute to my undertaking, but the City, and the people of England take my part very warmly, and I am told the best of the Citizens will give me proofs of it by their contributions.

In its published form *Polly* realized some £1,200, more than Gay could have hoped for had the play been produced.

The Duchess's contribution has been variously interpreted. Most critics have assumed that the £100 was merely a generous gesture on her part at the time subscriptions for the play were solicited. The Duchess Sarah, however, who placed the figure at '100 guineas', was quoted as saying that the money was in payment for Gay's *Epistle to Her Grace, Henrietta, Duchess of Marlborough* (1722). She characterized Gay as 'a very low poet that will tell her that she is what she knows she is not . . .'. See Mrs. Arthur Colville, *Duchess Sarah* (1904), p. 312.

I could talk to you a good deal more, but I am afraid I shall write too much for you, and for myself; I have not writ so much together since my sickness. I cannot omit telling you that Dr Arbuthnot's attendance and care of me show'd him the best of friends; Dr Hollings though entirely a stranger to me was join'd with him and us'd me the kindest and most handsome manner. Mr & Mrs Pulteney was greatly concern'd for me, visited me and show'd me the strongest proofs of friendship; when I see you, I will tell you of others as of Mr Pope, Mrs Blount, Mr and Mrs Rollinson, Lord and Lady Bolingbroke &c I think they are all your friends & well-Wishers I hope you will love them the better upon my account, but do not forget Mr Lewis nor Lord Bathurst, Sir W. Wyndham & Lord Gower, and Lord Oxford among the number.

From the Duke of Queensberry's / in Burlington Gardens. / March 18, 1728/9. / My service to Dr Delany & / Mr Stopfort.

Endorsement: Mr Gay. March 18 / 1728–9 [Swift's hand]

56. Gay *and the* Duke *and* Duchess of Queensberry *to* Mrs. Howard[1] 9 *August* [1729]

Add. 22626

[DUCHESS]   Middleton August the 9th:

My dear Mrs: Howard / you are resolved not to send the first Blot so you see I do, pray write somthing by the first opertunity, for tho I am as fully imployd as heart can wish, I find I have yet time to think of you I am surprisd you would not send me the good news of Lord Herberts[2] safe return &

---

[1] The year is inferred from the joint letter to Mrs. Howard of 27 August 1729 (Letter 57), which is dated in Gay's hand and places him at Middleton Stoney, the Queensberrys' hunting lodge in Oxfordshire, in August 1729.

[2] Henry Herbert (1693–1751), later 9th Earl of Pembroke, the 'architect earl', who is generally credited with designing Marble Hill. See *DNB* entry; see also *Earls*, pp. 79–92. Herbert's many eccentricities were a stock joke at Court, as the tone of the allusions to him in these letters suggests. A vegetarian and a fanatic on keeping fit, he had just returned from Paris where he startled the natives of that city by striding about the streets wearing a bag wig, in which

a great Deal of him, tho he has had nothing to say for himself, there must undoubtly be a great Deall to be sayd of him, what can be sayd for, his inhuman usage to so many persons of witt is past imagination. pray tell me if Mrs: Herbert[1] is in waiting if she is pray make her say any thing to me that she please's & pray to please me tell & tell me true that Mrs: Howard is perfectly well, now that I have indited, I think I cannot faill of your writing, unless you are very ungreatfull which I will never beleive till I have your own word for it / finis

I say somthing very obliging to Mrs: Meddows & Mrs: Cartrett Mr Gay Borrows the rest of the Papper for his use

[GAY] I think it may be of use to let you know that Middleton is near Bicester in Oxfordshire.

That blot was of my making and not on purpose / as witness. Queensberry.[2] Now you know every thing about the blot; Ile go on with my Letter. We do not play at Cards, & yet the days are too short for us, I know that this will scarce be credited yet it is true. We do not want one another's company, nor are we tir'd of one another, this too sounds a little incredible yet it is true. You see that we that live in the Country speak truth, and are willing that others should think we do so. I wish this may not be interpreted a reflection by somebody that does not understand it: so I will not say anymore about truth.

The Dutchess made these blots, and values herself upon it; I desire you would send word whether White currants be proper to make tarts, 'tis a point that we dispute upon every day, & will never be ended unless you decide it. The Dutchess would be extreamly glad if you could come here this day sevennight, but if you cannot; come this day fortnight at farthest, and bring as many unlikely people as you can to keep you company. Have you lain at Marble Hill since we left Petersum, if you had lain there, I believe we should not have left Petersum. Hath the Dutchess an Aunt

he carried a supply of watercress and beetroot. See Chesterfield to Mrs. Howard, 23 September 1729, *Suffolk Corr.* i. 366–7.

    [1] Mary Herbert, Bedchamber Woman

to the Queen and wife of the Hon. Robert Sawyer Herbert, Lord Herbert's younger brother.

    [2] The signature is in the Duke's hand.

Thanet alive again?[1] She says that there are but two people in the world that love & fear me, & those are Lord Drum & Lord Charles;[2] if they were awake I would make them Love those that I love, & say something civil to you. The Dutchess hath left off taking Snuff ever since you have, but she takes a little every day. I have not left it off and yet take none my resolution not being so strong. [DUKE] Tho you are a water drinker your self I dare say you will be sorry to hear that your freinds have strictly adhered to that liquor, for you may be sure their heads cannot be affected with that.

[GAY] General Dormer refus'd to eat a Wheatear because they call it here a Fern-Knacker, but since he knew twas a wheat'ear he is extreamly concern'd. You are desir'd to acquaint Mrs Smith that the Dutchess was upon the brink of leaving off painting the first week she came here, but hath since taken it up with great success; she hopes she will never think of her & my Lord Castlemain of the same day. The Duke hath rung the Bell for Supper, & says how can you write such stuff. & so we conclude,

> as tis fitting we shude, / for the sake of our food. / So dont think this rude / Would my name was / Gertrude. / or Simon & jude.

[DUKE] The writers of this, employ great part of their time in reading Les Contes Tartares[3] & like it extreamly, I mean the two principal writers—

[GAY] For my part I am forc'd to say I like them to flatter the Dutchess.

Duke Disney is not yet come to Mr Dormers, The Old Soldier is there, & can now lend you better Tea. There is a Cock Pheasant at Child-grove that is certainly a witch. Mr White cannot kill it though he shoots in a portuguese habit. There is a Gentleman that shall be nameless that hath

---

[1] 'This no doubt alludes to Mary Saville . . . wife of Sackville, who became on the 30th of July, 1729, seventh Earl of Thanet; but how any Lady Thanet was the duchess's aunt does not appear' —Croker, *Suffolk Corr.* i. 356, n. 4.

[2] The Queensberrys' sons, Henry, Earl of Drumlanrig, aged six, and Lord Charles Douglas, aged three.

[3] *Mille et un quarts d'heures, contes tartares* by Thomas-Simon Gueullette, a popular book of romantic tales similar to *Arabian Nights Entertainments*.

turn'd two or three brace of foxes into his Garden to prevent his being overstock'd with poultry. The Dutchess would not venture to keep a Peacock here, if any body would give her one. We liked our Mushrooms here very well till General Dormer told us they were tame ones.

[On verso of final sheet, in Duchess' hand] Whimsical / by several hands tis a pitty I should spell / pity with a double T / tis I say a pity that so much / plain paper should lye waste / we have a great Deal more / wit but no more time /

[Duke] there is proper care taken that this may / not be thought plain paper

57. Gay *and the* Duchess of Queensberry to Mrs. Howard *27 August 1729*

Add. 22626

Your Letter will be unanswerd because it is unanswerable[1] But notwithstanding that I was determind to write whether her Grace will or no as I told her just now as we were walking by Moonlight; we made several observations upon Clouds and Skies, which were you a painter might be of singular use to you, but they are not to be describd by words; perhaps you may see them some time hence upon vellom by her Grace's pencil. I desire you would not let Mrs Herbert know, that somebody[2] made a visit last night to Mrs Fermor after it was dark, it rain'd very hard indeed, and she had the good fortune to call her from prayers, so that Mrs Herbert, if she should ever come to know it, must allow it, in every respect a very regular and seasonable visit. The night before about the same hour the same person, made a visit to General Dormer who is so well recoverd of a fit of the Gout, that if he had provided himself with a large pair shoes he could have walk'd. To morrow we are to have the honour to see Lady Thanet; The Dutchess was ask'd a fortnight or three weeks ago to come to Asterop in the morning now and then to play at Hazard with that Lady, but she hath not com-

---

[1] Mrs. Howard's letter, apparently another 'Cheddar' letter, has been lost.
[2] The Duchess.

ply'd with it yet, perhaps if very bad weather should come on, it might be an inducement. Lord Drumlanrig read of an Entertainment at Marble Hill in the News-paper to night with a great deal of pleasure because he found your name mention'd; I tell you this, because I know you love Children and love to have children love you, [A sentence deleted here.] What is blotted out was nonsense, so that tis not worth while to try to read it. It was well meant; the Dutchess said it was very obscure, and I found out that it was not to be understood at all, nor by any alteration to be made intelligible, so out it went.

We have this afternoon been reading Polybius, we were mightily pleas'd with the Account of the Roman Wars with the Gauls, but we did not think his account of the Achaians, and his remarks upon the Historian Philargichus so entertaining, as for ought we knew it might be judicious. I know you will be very uneasy unless I tell you what picture the Dutchess hath in hand. Tis a round Landskip of Paul Brils which Mr Dormer lent her; in which there are figures very neatly finish'd. Tis larger than any she hath yet done; by the dead colouring I guess, (tho her Grace is not very sanguine) it will in the end turn out very well.

[DUCHESS] I dont understand which of our Correspondance this Letter is fit for, for there is neither witt, folly, or solid sense, nor no good foundation for noncence which is the only thing that I am well versd in. there was all these good things in the delightfull letter you sent us, but as all the diferent hands are not known they are unanswerable, for the future then pray sign or come, the later is Best, for whoever can write so well, must speak so. but now I think we had better allways write, for the good of posterity.

[GAY] Little did I think to have such an encomium upon my stile, for it certainly must be very particularly judicious, when a person could follow the manner of it, and write sense or nonsense as they lik'd best. For the future pray direct to us at Fox-warren hall;[1] we have lost so much poultry of late that the place henceforward is to take that name. The Duke

---

[1] See the preceding letter (Letter 56) for the Duke's alleged scheme of using foxes to prevent the overstocking of poultry.

is gone to Langley to Lady Dalkeith, who to night we heard is much better.[1] The Wind whistles, her Grace says it sounds like Amesbury, she shall she believes soon be in town for two or three days before she goes there for two or three year. If Dr Arbuthnot comes in your way Let him know, I wish him health, & offer him my service, I do the same to Mrs Blount & Mr Pope. Wherever I am I always shall wish to serve you, which next to being with you is one of the things in the world the most agreeable to me.

Aug. 27. 1729.

58. Gay *to* Swift 9 *November 1729*

Add. 4805

I have long known you to be my friend upon several occasions and particularly by your reproofs & admonitions. There is one thing which you have often put me in mind of, the over-running you with an answer before you had spoken, you find I am not a bit the better for it, for I still write & write on without having a word of an answer. I have heard of you once by Mr Pope; Let Mr Pope hear of you the next time by me. By this way of treating me, I mean by your not letting me know that you remember me you are very partial to me, I should have said very just to me; you seem to think that I do not want to be put in mind of you, which is very true, for I think of you very often and as often wish to be with you. I have been in Oxfordshire with the Duke of Queensberry for these three months, & have had very little correspondence with any of our Friends. I have employ'd my time in new-writing a damnd play which I writ sever[al] Years ago call'd the Wife of Bathe, as 'tis approv'd or disapprov'd of by my friends when I come to town I shall either have it acted or let it alone, if we[ak] Brethren do not take offence at it. The ridicule turns upon Supe[rsti]tion, & I have avoided the very words Bribery & corruption. Folly indeed is a word that I have venturd to make use of, but that is a term that never gave fools offence. Tis a common saying,

[1] Lady Jane Douglas, the Duke's sister, who had married the Earl of Dalkeith, died four days later, 31 August 1729. See GEC, ii. 368.

that he is wise that knows himself; what hath happen'd of late I think is a proof that it is not limited to the wise. My Lord Bathurst is still our Cashier, when I see him I intend to settle our accounts, & repay myself the five pou[nds] out of the two hundred that I owe you. Next week I believe I shall be in town. Not at Whitehall for those lodgings were judg'd not convenient for me & dispos'd of.[1] Direct to me at the Duke of Queensberrys in Burlington Gardens near Piccadilly. You have often twitted me in the teeth with hankering after the Court, in that you mistook me, for I know by experience that there is no dependance that can be sure but a dependance upon ones-self. I will take care of the little fortune I have got, I know you will take this resolution kindly; and you see my inclinations will make me write to you whether you will write to me or no. I am / Dear Sir / Yours most sincerely & / most affectionately. JG.

Middleton Stoney. Novemr. 9. 1729.

To the Lady I live with I owe my Life & fortune. Think of her with respect; value & esteem her as I do, & nevermore despise a Fork with three prongs. I wish too you would not eat from the point of your knife.[2] She hath so much goodness, virtue & generosity that if you knew her you would have a pleasure in obeying her as I do. She often wishes she had known you.

Address: To / The Revd Dr Swift Dean / of St Patrick's in / Dublin. / Ireland.
Postmark: 10/NO
Endorsement: Mr Gay / Nov. 9th. 1729 [Swift's hand]

59. Gay *to* Swift *3 March 1729/30*

Add. 4805

Dear Sir / I find you are determin'd not to write to me according to our old stipulation. Had I not been every post for some time in expectation to have heard from you I should

---

[1] *Persona non grata* at Court because of *Polly*, Gay was dispossessed of the apartment at Whitehall which was his perquisite as Commissioner of the Lottery.

[2] On Swift's table manners see also Letter 49; Swift to Gay, 10 November 1730, *Swift Corr*. iii. 417.

have wrote to you before to have let you know the present
state of your affairs, for I would not have you think me capable of neglecting yours whatever you think of me as to my
own. I have receivd 21l–13–4 interest from Lord Bathurst
for your 200l from Octr. 1727 to Xmas 1729 being two
years and two months at 5l p Cent. Lord Bathurst gave me
a note for your 200l again, & to allow interest for the same
dated January 15 1729/30. If you would have me dispose of
your money any other way, I shall obey your orders; Let me
know what I shall do with the interest money I have receiv'd.
What I have done for you I did for myself, which will be always
the way of my transacting any thing for you. My old vamp'd
Play got me no money, for it had no success.[1] I am going
very soon into Wiltshire with the D[uke] of Queensberry
with intention to stay there till the winter; since I had that
severe fit of sickness[2] I find my health requires it, for I cannot bear the town as I could formerly, I hope another Summer's Air & exercise will reinstate me. I continue to drink
nothing but water, so that you cannot require any Poetry
from me; I have been very seldom abroad since I came to
town, & not once at Court; this is no restraint upon me, for
I am grown old enough to wish for retirement. I saw Mr
Pope a day or two ago in good Spirits, & with good wishes
for you, for we always talk of you; the Doctor does the same.
I have left off all great folks but our own family; perhaps you
will think all great folks little enough to leave off us in our
present situation. I dont hate the world but I laugh at it; for
none but fools can be in earnest about a trifle. / I am Dear
Sir / Yours most affectionately.

London. March. 3. 1729/30.

direct to me at the D. of Q. in Burlington Gardens.

Address: To / The Revd Dr Swift Dean / of St Patricks in / Dublin /
Ireland.
Postmark: 3/MR
Endorsement: Mar. 3d. 1729–30 / Mr Gay / About money in / Lord
Bathurst's hands / Mr. Gay. Mar. 3d. 1729–30 / Answred. Mar.
19th [Swift's hand]

----

[1] The revised version of *The Wife of Bath* was produced at the Theatre Royal,
Lincoln's Inn Fields, on 19 January 1730.   [2] In the winter of 1728/9.

60. Gay *to* Swift *31 March 1730*

Add. 4805

Dear Sir. / I expect in about a fortnight to set out for
Wiltshire, & am as impatient as you seem to be to have me,
to get a horseback; I thought proper to give you this intelligence because Mr Lewis told me last sunday that he was in
a day or two to set out for the Bath, so that very soon you are
like to have neither of your Cashiers in town. Continue to
direct to me at this House, the Letters will be sent to me
wherever I am. My Ambition at present is levell'd to the same
point that you direct me to, for I am every day building
Villakins, and have given over that of Castles.[1] If I were to
undertake it in my present circumstance, I should in the
most thrifty Scheme soon be straiten'd; & I hate to be in
debt, for I cannot bear to pawn five pounds worth of my
liberty to a Taylor or a Butcher; I grant you this is not having
the true spirit of modern Nobility, but tis hard to cure the
prejudice of education. I have made your compliments to
Mr P[2] who is very much your humble servant. I have not
seen the Doctor, & am not like to see his Roan Brother[3] very
soon for he is gone to China. Mr Pope told me he had acquainted the Doctor with the misfortune of the Sour Hermitage, My Lord Oxford told me He at present could match
yours & from the same person. The Doctor was touch'd
with your disappointment & hath promis'd to represent this
affair to his Brother at his return from China. I assure you
too for all your gibes, that I wish you heartily good wine
though I can drink none myself. When Lord Bolingbroke is
in town he lodges at Mr Chetwynd's in Dover Street, I do
not know how to direct to him in the Country. I have been
extreamly taken up of late in settling a Steward's Account. I
am endeavouring to do all the justice & service I can for a

[1] Swift had expressed the wish that
Gay might establish himself in a 'little
Villakin' in Twickenham near Pope. See
Swift to Gay, 19 March 1729/30, *Swift
Corr.* iii. 381. See also Gay's inquiries
about the 'widow's house'(Letters 53, 61).

[2] Pulteney.

[3] Robert Arbuthnot, a banker, had
offices in Rouen and Paris. He had sent
Swift 150 bottles of wine which soured
unaccountably.

friend, so I am sure you will think I am well employ'd. Upon
this occasion I now & then have seen Jo Taylor, who says
he hath a demand upon you for Rent, you having taken his
house in the Country, & he being determin'd not to let it to
any body else; and he thinks it but reasonable that you should
either come & live in it or pay your rent. I neither ride nor
walk but I design to do both this month & to become a laudable practitioner. The Dutchess wishes she had seen you &
thinks you were in the wrong to hide yourself and peep
through the window that day she came to Mr Popes. The
Duke too is oblig'd to you for your good opinion & is your
humble servant. If I were to write, I am afraid I should again
incurr the displeasure of my superiors, for I cannot for my
life think so well of them as they themselves think they
deserve. If you have a very great mind to please the
Dutchess and at the same time to please me, I wish you
would write a Letter to her to send to her Brother Lord
Cornbury to advise him in his travells, for she says she would
take your advice rather than mine, and she remembers that
you told her in the Park that you lov'd & honour'd her
family.[1] You always insisted upon a Lady's making advances
to you; I do not know whether you will think this declaration
sufficient. Then too when you were in England she writ a
Letter to you, & I have been often blam'd since for not
delivering it. The day the Pension Bill was thrown out of
the House of Lords Lord Bathurst spoke with great applause. I have not time to go to Mr Pope's; in a day or two
very probably I shall see him & acquaint him about the
Usquebagh.[2] I will not imbezzle your interest money though
by looking upon accounts I see how money may be im-
bezzled; as to my being engag'd in an affair of this kind, I
say nothing for myself, but that I will do all I can, for the
rest I leave Jo Taylor to speak for me. today I dine with
Alderman Barbar the present Sheriff who holds his feast in
the city. Does not Chartres' misfortunes grieve you, for that

---

[1] Swift had evidently once met the
Duchess when she was a child. See Swift
to Gay, 10 November 1730, *Swift Corr.*
iii. 417.

[2] *Usquebaugh*, Irish and Scottish
Gaelic, literally 'water of life', from
which the modern word 'whisky'
evolved. See *NED*. Swift had written to
Gay that he had sent several bottles
to Pope consigned to Bathurst (Swift to
Gay, 19 March 1729/30, *Swift Corr.*
iii. 381).

great man is like to save his life and lose some of his money, a very hard case!

I am just now come from the Alderman's Feast, who had a very fine dinner & a very fine Appearance of Company. the Post is just going away.

March. 31. 1730.

Address: To the Reverend / Dr Swift Dean of St / Patrick's in Dublin / Ireland.
Postmark: 31/MR
Endorsement: Mr Gay. Mar. 31st. 1730. [Swift's hand]

61. Gay *to* Mrs. Howard *9 May 1730*

Add. 22626

Madam / Tis what the Dutchess never would tell me so that is impossible for me to tell you how she does; but I cannot take it ill, for I really believe 'tis what she never really and truly did to any body in her life. as I am no Physician & cannot do her any good, one would wonder how she could refuse to answer this question out of common civility, but she is a profess'd hater of common civility, and so I am determin'd never to ask her again. If you have a mind to know what she hath done since she came here, the most material things that I know of is, that she hath work'd a rose[1] & milk'd a Cow, and those two things I assure you are of more consequence I verily believe than hath been done by any body else. Mrs Herbert was very angry with her Grace the night before she left the town, that she could part with her friends with such an indecent cheerfullness; she wishes she had seen you at the same time, that she might have known whether she could have carry'd this happy indifference for the world through or no. She is grown a great Admirer of two Characters in Prior's Poems, that of Sauntering Jack & idle Joan,[2] & she thinks them Persons worthy imitation; At

[1] In needle point.
[2] 'An Epitaph' (1718). Sauntering Jack and Idle Joan, who are described as neither 'Good, nor Bad, nor Fools, nor Wise', spent their days in complete indolence. For the French original of this piece see Boswell, *Life of Johnson*, eds. G. B. Hill and L. F. Powell, iii. 533.

this very instant she herself is in their way; she had a mind to write to you, but cannot prevail with herself to set about it; she is now thinking of Mrs Herbert, but is too indolent to tell me to make her compliments to her; just this minute she is wishing you were in this very room, but she will not give herself the trouble to say so to me, all that I know of it is, she looks all this, for she knows I am writing to you; there is indeed a very good reason for her present indolence, for she is looking upon a book which she seems to be reading, but I believe the same page hath lain open before her ever since I began this letter. Just this moment she hath utter'd these words, that she will take it as a very great favour that you would speak to Mrs Herbert to speak to Lord Herbert that he would speak to any body who may chance to go by Mr Nix's house to call upon him to hasten his sending the peice of furniture which perhaps as soon as she receives may tempt her Grace to write to somebody or other that very little expects it, for she loves to do things by surprise. She would take it kindly if you would write to her against this thing comes here, for I verily believe she will try whether or no it be convenient for writing,[1] and perhaps she may make the tryal to you; she did not bid me say this, but as she talks of you often I think you have a fair chance.

As soon as you are settled at Marble Hill, I beg you to take the Widows House for me,[2] & persuade the Dutchess to come to Petersham. But wherever you are at present I can only wish to be with you, do what you can for me & let me hear from you, 'till the Dutchess writes to you, you may write to me, and if you express any resentment against her for not writing to you I will let her know it in what manner you shall please to direct me. I beg you to make my compliments to Mrs Blount, & Dr Arbuthnot. I wish'd to see Mr Pope oftener than I did, Let him know that I will write to him soon, & you will much oblige me.

May 9th. 1730.

[1] The Duchess was expecting some new chairs for which she was making coverings. See also Letter 63; Mrs. Howard to Gay, 31 July [1730], *Suffolk Corr*. i. 376.

[2] See also Letters 53, 60.

62. Gay *to* Swift *4 July 1730*

Add. 4805

Dear Sir. / You tell me that I have put myself out of the way of all my old acquaintance, so that unless I hear from you I can know nothing of you; is it not barbarous then to leave me so long without writing one word to me? If you wont write to me for my sake, methinks you might write for your own. How do you know what is become of your money? If you had drawn upon me when I expected it you might have had your money, for I was then in town; but I am now at Amesbury near Salisbury in Wiltshire at the Duke of Queensberry's; the Dutchess sends you her services; I wish you were here, I fancy you would like her, and the Place; you might fancy yourself at home, for we have a Cathedral near us, where you might find a Bishop of the same name.[1] You might ride upon the Downs & write conjectures upon Stonhenge. We are but five & twenty miles from the Bath, and I was told this very Evening by General Dormer who is here that he heard somewhere or other that you had some intentions of coming there the latter Season; I wish any thing would bring us together but your want of health. I have left off wine & writing, for I really think that man must be a bold writer who trusts to Wit without it. I took your Advice, & some time ago took to Love, & made some advances to the Lady you sent me to in Soho,[2] but I met no return, so I have given up all thoughts of it, & have now no pursuit or Amusement. A State of indolence is what I dont like; tis what I would not chuse; I am not thinking of a Court or perferment, for I think the Lady I live with is my friend, so that I am [at] the height of my ambition. You have often told me, there is a time of life that every one wishes for some settlement of his own; I have frequently that feeling about me; but I fancy it will hardly ever be my Lot; so that I will endeavour to pass away Life as agreeably as I can in the

---

[1] Dr. Benjamin Hoadly was then Bishop of Salisbury and his brother, John, Archbishop of Dublin.

[2] Mrs. Drelincourt, widow of Peter Drelincourt, Dean of Armagh. Gay called on her infrequently and his courting was, at best, perfunctory. Swift called him 'the Sillyest lover in Christendom' (Swift to Gay, 29 June 1731, *Swift Corr.* iii. 471).

way I am. I often wish to be with you or you with me, & I believe you think I say true. I am determin'd to write to you, though those dirty fellows of the Post office do read my Letters, for since I saw you I am grown of that consequence to be Obnoxious to the men I despise; so that it is very probable in their hearts they think me an honest man. I have heard from Mr Pope but once since I left London, I was sorry I saw him so seldom but I had business that kept me from him.[1] I often wish we were together again. If you will not write, come. I am, Dear Sir / Yours most sincerely & / affectionately.

Amesbury near Salisbury in / Wiltshire. July. 4. 1730.

Endorsement: Mr Gay. / Jul. 3d. 1730 [Swift's hand]

63. Gay *and the* Duchess of Queensberry *to* Mrs. Howard *20 August 1730*

Add. 22626

[DUCHESS] it was not that I hated writing my Dear Mrs Howard (that I hope & think I never shall to you) but violent pain in my face & Ear, that did & only could hinder me from thanking you for your most wellcome Letter. this entertainment I have had constantly at an hour for these three Evenings successively, & am not now without a strong hint of a fresh supply of pain I believe I got it by taking care of my self (as they call it) by taking the Air in a Phaeton like Lord Tankerville,[2] one ought to suffer who can do any thing like him—because sure never to come up to the original. I like the account you give of your Health, I dont know how you may like what I have to say of mine, but all that I know is—that it has been & may be worse, & that I dont in the least suspect that it will ever be Better, & if I am contented I think you must allow this to be in a tollerable good Situation[.]

[1] The settlement of the Steward's account for the Duke of Queensberry. See Letter 60.

[2] Charles Bennet, 2nd Earl of Tan-kerville, who was instrumental in introducing Stephen Duck's poetry to the Court. See Lewis Melville, *Maids of Honour* (1927), p. 132.

[GAY] The Dutchess says she can't say a word more if I would give her the world, & that her misery hath got the better of her pleasure in writing to you. She thanks you for your information, & says, that if she can bear herself, or think that any body else can she intends to make her visit next week; now it is my opinion that she need never have any scruples of this kind, but as to herself you know she hath often an unaccountable way of thinking; & say what you will to her, she will now & then hear you, but she will always think & act for herself. I have been waiting three or four minutes for what she hath to say, & at last she tells me she cannot speak one word more, & at the same time is so very unreasonable as to desire you would write her a long Letter, as she knows you love it. I have several complaints to make to you of her treatment, but I shall only mention the most barbarous of 'em. She hath absolutely forbid her Dog to be fond of me, & takes all occasions to snubb her if she shows me the least civility. How do you think Lord Herbert would take such usage from you or any Lady in Christendom? Now she says, I must write you a long Letter, but to be sure I cannot say what I would about her because she is looking over me as I write. If I should [say] any good of her I know she would not like it; and I have said my worst of her already. The Chairs go on with great diligence & application, & if you please to come & sit down you may take your choice of two or three, & she says just now that she hath a particular reason for your coming, for you will be in a more poetical situation sitting upon a groupe of flowers, than hoydening a horseback in a croud,[1] & your verses shall be ready as soon as I see the theme. She is in prodigious haste to have this done, that afterwards I may describe her in her flannel veil.

[DUCHESS] as for My Lady Essex &c I am quite passive but if you could send me word that my Lord had a broken head, I should think it had receivd its only due reward.[2]

---

[1] Writing from Windsor on 31 July, Mrs. Howard expressed her distaste for the 'noise and violence' of the Royal Hunt. See *Suffolk Corr.* i. 376. See also Pope to the Misses Blount, 13 September 1717, *Pope Corr.* i. 427.

[2] Lady Essex is, of course, Essex's second wife, Elizabeth Russell, and not his first Countess, Jane Hyde, the Duchess's sister.

[GAY] We wonder we have heard nothing from Mr Bridgeman, if you chance to see him pray tell him so.

As for the person that you are so sanguine about his long life I know him to be a very complaisant Gentleman, & the Dutchess thinks him so heroic that he will not desire to live toe long, when his honour may suffer by it. The patterns that Mr Wheeler hath just now sent us we dont approve of, so that I am going to try to make a Sketch to send him for his better information.

[DUCHESS] dont think I am lazy & so have fram'd an excuse for I am realy in pain (at some Moments intolerable since this was began) I think often I could be mighty glad to see you & tho you deserve vastly, thats saying much from me (for I can bear to be alone) & upon all accounts—think I am much better here than any where else. I think here to go on & prosper mighty prettily, & like the habitation so well (that if I could in nature otherways be forgitfull) that would put me in mind of what I owe to those who helpt me on to where I would be—sooner than I feard I could be—pray tell Mrs: Meddows that I was in hopes she would have made a dutyfull visit to her father, if any one elce care for my respects they may accept of them, I will present 'em to Lord Herbert whether he care or not, I hope by this time he is able to carry himself & Fop where ever he pleases[1]—if I had the same power over you I would not writ you word that I am yours &c, but since I can only write—beleive that I am

---

[1] The reference to Fop raises some questions. Mrs. Howard had a dog of this name whom Ault identified as the addressee of the celebrated 'Bounce to Fop. An Heroick Epistle from a Dog at Twickenham to a Dog at Court' (*New Light*, p. 345; *Minor Poems*, pp. 370–1). Ault, however, failed to take into account why Pope, who was always favourably disposed toward Mrs. Howard, should satirize her in *this* poem. The Duchess's remark, together with Chesterfield's two references to Herbert's dog by name (to Mrs. Howard, 13 July [1728], *Suffolk Corr.* i. 303; and 21 October [1728], ibid. i. 329), establishes another dog at Court named Fop, whose master was a natural target for satire. Pope would undoubtedly have encountered Fop and the quixotic Herbert while assisting with the landscaping at Marble Hill. A second difficulty with Ault's thesis is that the context of 'Bounce to Fop' makes it clear that Fop's owner is a male.

Your pilf'ring Lord, with simple Pride,
May wear a Pick-lock at his Side;
My Master wants no Key of State,
For *Bounce* can keep his House and Gate.

These lines receive considerable illumination if it is recalled that Herbert was then Lord of the Bedchamber.

to you every thing—that you have ever read att the Bottom of a letter, but not that I am so only by way of conclusion—
The 20th: of August / 1730

64. Gay *and the* Duchess of Queensberry *to* Mrs. Howard¹ *11 September* [*1730*]

Add. 22626

Madam / I cannot neglect this opportunity of writing to you & begging you to be a Mediator between my Lady Dutchess & me we having at present a quarrel about a Fishing-rod, & at the same time to give her your Opinion whether you think it proper for her to stay here till after Christmas, for I find that neither Place nor preferment will let me leave here, & when she hath been long enough in one place, prevail with her if you can to go to another. I would always have her do what she will because I am glad to be of her Opinion, & because I know tis what I must always do myself.

[Duchess] To follow ones fancy is by much the best medicine it has quite cur'd my face & left me no pain but the imposibility of being in to places at once which is no small sorrow sence one of them would make me near you. I am not sure that, as the least Evil you would chouse that, & that you bless yourself that the fool could realy think you car'd to hear from her—I know no news yet of Mrs: harbert The Boy's & I are to lean to travel as yet. compasion being the predominate pashion of the place we are preserv'd alive with as much care as the partriges which no one yet has had the [least?] heart to kill tho' severall Barbarous attempts have been made if I could write I would for ever but my pen is so much your freind that itt will only let me tell you that I am extreamly so

¹ The year is established by the Duchess's reference to her headaches (see Letter 63) and the plans to spend Christmas at Amesbury (see Letter 66). September 11 was a Friday in 1730 but the Duchess's reliability as to dates is questionable.

I pray it may not be so dificult for My Dear Mrs howard to forgive us to read this provokation, by the next I hope to write plain

Sept: the 11th: / Saterday

65. Gay *and the* Duchess of Queensberry *to* Swift
8 November 1730

Add. 4806

Dear Sir. / So you are determin'd never to write to me again, but for all that you shall not make me hold my tongue; you shall hear from me (the Post office willing) whether you will or no. I see none of the Folks you correspond with, so that I am forc'd to pick up intelligence concerning you as I can, which hath been so very little, that I am resolv'd to make my complaints to you as a friend who I know love to relieve the distress'd; and in the circumstances I am in, where should I apply but to my best friend? Mr Pope indeed, upon my frequent enquirys hath told me that the Letters that are directed to him concern me as much as himself, but what you say of yourself, or of me, or to me I know nothing at all. Lord Carteret was here yesterday in his return from the Isle of Wight where he had been a Shooting; & left 7 pheasants with us. He went this morning to the Bath to Lady Carteret who is perfectly recover'd. He talk'd of you for three hours last night, & told me that you talk of me; I mean that you are prodigiously in his favour, as he says, & I believe that I am in yours; for I know you to be a just & equitable person, and tis but my due. He seem'd to take to me, which I take to proceed from your recommendation; though indeed there is another reason for it, for he is now out of Employment,[1] and my friends have generally been of that sort; for I take to them as being naturally inclin'd to those who can do no mischief. Pray, do you come to England this year, he thinks you do, I wish you would & so does the Dutchess

---

[1] Carteret had been dismissed from his post as Lord-Lieutenant of Ireland in April.

of Queensberry. What would you have more to induce you?
Your Money crys come spend me; and your friends cry
come see me. I have been treated barbarously by you; if you
knew how often I talk of you, how often I think of you, you
would now & then direct a Letter to me, & I would allow
Mr Pope to have his share in it, in short I dont care to keep
any Man's money that serves me so; Love or money I must
have, & if you will not let me have the comfort of the one, I
think I must endeavour to get a little comfort by spending
some of the other. I must beg that you would call at Amesbury in your way to London, for I have many things to say
to you, & I can assure you, you will be welcome to a three
prong'd fork. I remember your prescription, & I do ride upon
the Downs, and at present I have no Asthma; I have kill'd
five brace of Partridges, & four Brace & a half of Quails, &
I do not Envy either Sir Robert, or Stephen Duck who is the
favorite Poet of the Court. I hear sometimes from Mr Pope,
& from scarce any body else; Were I to live here never so
long I believe I should never think of London, but I cannot
help thinking of you. Were you here, I could talk to you, but
I would not, for you shall have all your share of talk which
was never allow'd you at Twickenham. You know this was a
grievance you often complain'd of, & so in revenge you make
me write all, & answer nothing. I beg you my compliments
to Dr Delany. I am Dear Sir, / Yours most Affectionately. /
JG.

Amesbury near Salisbury in / Wiltshire.

Novr. 8. 1730.

I ended the Letter as above to go to the Dutchess, & she
told me I might go down & come a quarter of an hour hence;
I had a design to have ask'd her to have sign'd the invitation
that I have made you as I dont know how much she may have
to say to you, I think it will be prudent to leave off that she
may not be stinted for want of room. So much I will say, that
whether she signs it or no, both the Duke & Dutchess would
be very glad you would come to Amesbury; & you must be
persuaded that I say this without the least private view; for
what is it to me whether you come or no? for I can write to
you, you know.

[DUCHESS] I would fain have you come, I cannot say you'll be wellcome—for I dont know you, & perhaps I shall not like you, but if I do not—(unless you are a very vain person) you shall know my thoughts as soon as I do myself—CQ

Endorsement: Mr Gay, and Dutchess / of Queensbury / Nov. 8th. 1730 [Swift's hand]

66. Gay *and the* Duchess of Queensberry *to* Swift
6 December 1730

Add. 4806

Dear Sir. / Both your Letters to my great satisfaction I have receiv'd; You were mistaken as to my being in town for I have been here ever since the beginning of May; but the best way is to direct my Letters always to the Duke's house in London; and they are sent hither by his Porter. We shall stay here till after the Holidays; you say we deserve Envy, I think we do, for I envy no man either in town or out of it; We have had some few Visiters and every one of 'em such that one would desire to visit; the Dutchess is a more severe check upon my finances than even you were and I submit, as I did to you, to comply to my own good; I was a long time before I could prevail with her to let me allow myself a pair of shoes with two heels, for I had lost one, and the shoes were so decayd that they were not worth mending; you see by this that those who are the most generous of their own can be the most covetous for others; I hope you will be so good to me as to use your interest with her, (for whatever she says, you seem to have some) to indulge me with the extravagance suitable to my fortune. The Lady you mention that dislikes you hath no discernment,[1] I really think you may safely venture to Amesbury, though indeed the Lady here likes to have her own way as well as you which may sometimes occasion disputes, and I tell you beforehand that I cannot take your part, I think her so often in the right, that you will have great difficulty to persuade me she is in the wrong; then there is another thing

[1] The Queen.

I ought to tell you to deterr you from this place, which is, that the Lady of the house is not given to show civility to those she does not like; she speaks her mind, and loves truth; for the uncommonness of the thing I fancy your curiosity will prevail over your fear & you will like to see such a Woman. but I say no more, till I know whether her Grace will fill up the rest of the Paper.

[DUCHESS] write I must; particularly now as I have an oppertunity to indulge my predominant passion contradiction, I do in the first place contradict most things Mr: Gay says of me—to deterr you from coming here which if you ever do I hereby assure you that unless I like my own way better you shall have yours, & in all disputes you shall convince me if you can. but by what I see of you this is not a misfortune that will allways happen for I find you are a great Mistaker, for example you take prudence for imperiousness tis from [this] first that I determind not to like one who is too gid[dy h]eaded—for me to be certain whether or no I shall ever be acquainted with, I have often known people take great delight in Building Castles in the Air. but I should chuse to Build friends upon a more Solide foundation. I would fain know you—for I often hear more good likeable things than tis possible any one can deserve. pray come that I may find out somthing wrong, for I, and I bileive most women have an inconceivable pleasure to find out any faults —except their own—Mr Cibber is made Poet Laureat. I am Sir as much your Humble: Servant as I can be to any person I dont know / CQ

Mr: Gay is very / peevish that I spell & write ill but I dont care for the pen nor I can do no better besides I think you have flatterd me & such people ought to be put to trouble.

[GAY] Now I hope you are pleas'd; and that you will allow for so small a summ as 200l you have a lumping penniworth.[1]

Amesbury. Decr. 6. 1730.

[1] In his letter of 19 November Swift had admonished Gay for leaving the Duchess room for only three lines in their last letter and professed he would have given the £200 which Gay was keeping for him for three lines more. See *Swift Corr.* iii. 421.

Address: For / The Reverend Dr Swift / Dean of St Patrick's in /
   Dublin / Ireland / by way of London
Postmark: 7/DE
Endorsements: [In Swift's hand] Decbr. 14th. 1730. Mr Gay.— /
            and D——s of Q——y Mr Gay, and
            / D——s of Q——y. / Decbr. 6th.
            1730 / Answered

67. Gay *and the* Duchess of Queensberry *to* Mrs. Howard[1] [*18 December 1730*]

Add. 22626

[DUCHESS] My Dear Mrs: Howard you cannot imagin in
what Due time your Letter came for I had given you up, &
with great pains had very near brought our freind Mr: Gay
to own that no body cared for us, & a few more thoughts
which shall now be namless. I am sincerly sorry that you have
been ill, & very very glad that you are better & think of life
for I know none who one could more wish to have live than
yourself. I dont in the least approve of your changing your
way of thinking of me, for I was convincd t'was a good one,
& when such opinions change tis seldome for the better.
if it could on my account I declare you'd be in the wrong, for
to my knowledge I improve in no one thing. the best thing
I can say for my self is that I feel no allteration in the regard
& inclination I have toe you. I have no comprehension what
I said in my letter but at that time my Body was distemper'd
& very likely my mind also—yours at all times I know nothing of coming to Town I only know that when I do I shall
not be sorry to see you & this is knowing a great deal, for I
shall not be glad to come & shall only come if it be unavoid-
able this is blunt truth I own t'would look less like indifference if I had writ some sivill lie

[GAY] Every thing that is above written is so plain & clear
that it needs no comment; the writer I know to be so strictly
addicted to truth that I believe every word of it; if it is not

---

[1] The dating is from the postmark and Mrs. Howard's endorsement.

writ in the fashionable expression, I conclude you will impute [it] to her manner. She was really concernd very much, that after we knew you were ill, we were so long before we could get a letter from you; Let her contradict this if she can. You tell her you are riding for your life, I fancy she would do it too for yours though she will not for her own. I believe she will not like that I should say any thing more about her, so that I shall leave you to your own thoughts about what she hath said herself, for I find she does not much care to be talk'd to, and as little likes to be talk'd of. if she writes truth I hope she will allow me the liberty to do the same. I find it a very hard thing to write upon this sheet of paper, for I fancy she hath writ on purpose to puzzle me as well as you, I have sometimes a great mind to answer the above Letter, but I know she will do what she will do, and as little as she likes herself, she likes her own advice better than any bodys else, and that is a reason in my opinion that should prevail with her to take more care of herself; I just before said I would say no more upon this subject, but if I don't lay down the pen, I find I can't help it. I have no desire to c[ome] to town at all, for if I were there I can't see you,[1] so that unless she turns me away I am fixt for Life at Amesbury. So that to every thing that relates to me I referr you to her Letter.

Address: To the Honble: Mrs: Howard / Bed-Chamber Woman to the Queen / att her Lodgings / In St: James House / London
Postmark: 18/DE
Endorsement: The 19th: of Decbr. / 1730 [Mrs. Howard's hand]

68. Gay *to* Swift *20 March 1730/1*

Add. 4806

Dear Sir. / I think 'tis above 3 months ago that I wrote to you in partnership with the Dutchess. About a fortnight since I wrote to you from Twickenham for Mr Pope and myself,[2] he was then disabled from writing by a severe rheumatic

---

[1] In view of *Polly*, Gay was no longer welcome at St. James's Palace.

[2] Swift mentions a letter from Gay and Pope dated 25 February (see Swift to Gay and the Duchess, 13 March 1730/1, *Swift Corr.* iii. 445) but it has apparently been lost.

pain in his arm but is now pretty well again and at present in town. Lord Oxford, Lord Bathurst, He & I din'd yesterday at Barnes with old Jacob Tonson where we drank your Health. I am again by the advice of Physicians grown a moderate Wine drinker after an abstinence of above two years, and I now look upon myself qualified for society as before.

I formerly sent you a state of the Account between us. Lord B[1] this day hath payd me your principal & interest; the interest amounted to twelve pounds; and I want your directions How to dispose of the principal which must lye dead 'till I receive your orders. I had a Scheme of buying Lottery Tickets for you & keeping your principal entire; and as all my good fortune is to come, to show you that I consult your advantage, I will buy two more for myself, and you and I will go halves in the ten thousand pounds. That there will be a Lottery is certain, the Scheme is not yet declar'd, but I hear it will not be the most advantagious one for we are to have but 3 p Cent. I sollicit for no Court favours so that I propose to buy the tickets at the market price when they come out,[2] which will not be these two or three months. If you do not like to have your money thus dispos'd of, or if you like to trust to your own fortune rather than to share in mine Let me have your orders, and at the same time tell me what I shall do with the principal Summ.

I came to town the 7th of January last with the Duke & Dutchess about business for a fortnight, as it depended upon others we could not get it done 'till now. Next week we return to Amesbury in Wiltshire for the rest of the year; But the best way is always to direct to me at the Duke's in Burlington Gardens near Piccadilly. I am order'd by the Dutchess to grow rich in the manner of Sir John Cutler;[3] I have nothing at this present writing but my Frock that was made at Salisbury and a Bob perriwig. I persuade myself that it is shilling weather as seldom as possible[4] and have found out that there are few Court visits that are worth a

---

[1] Bathurst.

[2] This was Gay's last year as Commissioner of the Lottery. For Swift's reaction to investing his interest money in lottery tickets, see Swift to Bath-urst, 17 July 1731, *Swift Corr.* iii. 473.

[3] See Pope's *Epistle to Bathurst*, ll. 315–34.

[4] Inclement weather, requiring a one-shilling fare for a hackney coach.

shilling. in short I am very happy in my present indepen-
dency, I envy no man, but have the due contempt for the
voluntary slaves of Birth and fortune. I have such a Spite
against you that I wish you may long for my company as I
do for yours; though you never write to me you cannot make
me forget you, so that if it is out of friendship you write so
seldom to me it doth not answer the purpose. Those, who
you would like should remember you, do so, whenever I see
'em. I believe they do it upon their own account, for I know
few people who are solicitous to please or flatter me. The
Dutchess sends you her compliments & so would many
more if they knew of my writing to you.

March 20. 1730/1

Address: To / The Revd Dr Swift / Dean of St Patrick's in / Dublin. /
Ireland
Postmark: 20/MR
Endorsement: Mr Gay. / Mar. 20th. 1730–1 / Ansd. Apr. 13th. /
1731 [Swift's hand]

69. Gay *and the* Duchess of Queensberry *to* Swift

11 April 1731

Add. 4806

Dear Sir. / The fortune of the person you interest yourself
in, amounts to at present (all debts paid) above three thous-
and, four hundred pounds, so that, whatever other people
think, I look upon him, as to fortune, to be a happy that is
to say an independant creature. I have been in expectation
post after post to have receiv'd your directions about the
disposal of your money which Lord B[1] paid into my hands
some time ago: I left that sum with two hundred of my own
in Mr Hoare's hands[2] at my coming out of town. I shall go
to town for a few days very soon; if I hear nothing from you,
I will do with it as I do with my own. I made you a proposal
about purchasing Lottery tickets in partnership with myself,
that is to say, four tickets between us; this can be done with

---

[1] Bathurst.
[2] Henry Hoare of Stourhead, Wilt-shire, banker and grandson of Sir

Richard Hoare, founder of Hoare's
Bank and one-time Lord Mayor of
London.

overplus, with the interest money I have receiv'd, but in this I will do nothing till I hear from you. I am now got to my residence at Amesbury, getting health & saving money. Since I have got over the impediment to a writer of water-drinking, if I can persuade myself that I have any wit, & find I have inclination I intend to write, though as yet I have another impediment for I have not provided myself with a Scheme. Ten to one but I shall have a propensity to write against Vice, & who can tell how far that may offend? But an Author should consult his genius rather than his interest, if he cannot reconcile 'em. Just before I left London, I made a visit to Mrs Barber, I wish I could any ways have contributed to her subscription;[1] I have always found myself of no consequence & am now of less than ever; but I have found out a way in one respect, of making myself of more consequence, which is by considering other people of less. Those who have given one [me?] up, I have given up, & in short I seek after no friendships, but am content with what I have in the house, & they have subscrib'd; I propos'd it before Jo Taylor, who, upon hearing she was a friend of yours, offer'd his subscription & desir'd his compliments to you. I believe she hath given you an account that she hath some prospect of success from others recommendations to those I know, and I have not been wanting upon all occasions to put in my good word, which I fear avails but little. Two days ago I receiv'd a Letter from Dr Arbuthnot which gave me but a bad account of Mr Pope's health, I have writ to him but have not heard from him since I came into the country. If you knew the pleasure you gave me you would keep your contract of writing more punctually, & especially you would have answerd my last Letter, as it was about a money affair, & you have to do with a man of business. Your Letter was more to the Dutchess than to me, so I now leave off, to offer her the paper.

[Duchess] it was Mr: Gay's fault that I did not write sooner, which if I had I hope you would have been here by this time, for I have to tell you that all your articles are agreed

---

[1] Mary Barber, a Dublin poetess sponsored by Swift, was then in London seeking subscriptions for a volume of her poems. See *DNB* entry. Gay was a subscriber to Mrs. Barber's *Poems on Several Occasions* (1734).

to¹ & that I only love my own way when I meet not with others, whose ways I like better, I am in great hopes that I shall approve of yours, for to tell you the truth I am at present a little tir'd of my own. I have not a clear or a distinct voice, except when I am angry, but I am a very good Nurse when people do [not] fancy them selves sick, Mr: Gay knows this, & he knows too how to play att Backgammon. whether the Parson of the parish can I know not but if he cannot hold his tongue I can—pray sett out the first fair wind & stay with us as long as ever you please. I cannot name any fixt time that I shall like to maintain you & your equipage. but if I dont happen to like you I know I can so far govern my temper as to Endure you for about five days, so come away directly for at all hazards you'll be alow'd a good Breathing time. I shall make no sort of respectfull conclusion for till I know you I cannot tell what / I am to you

[GAY] The direction is to the Duke of Queensberrys in Burlington Gardens in Piccadilly; now I have told you this you have no excuse from writing but one which is coming. Get over your Lawsuit² & receive your money. [DUCHESS] he shall not write a word more / Aprill the 11th: 1731

from Amresbury in wiltshire

your Groom was mistaken for the house is big Enough,³ but the Parke is too Little

Address: To / The Revd Dr Swift Dean / of St Patrick's in / Dublin / Ireland / by London
Postmark: 12/AP
Endorsement: Mr Gay and / D——s of Q——y / Rx Apr. 20th 1731 [Swift's hand]

¹ Swift's 'conditions' for making a visit to Amesbury. See Swift to Gay and the Duchess, 13 March 1730/1, *Swift Corr.* iii. 445. The Duchess answers them point by point.

² Swift was involved in a seemingly interminable litigation to recover some £1,600. See Swift to Pope, 26 February 1729/30, *Swift Corr.* iii. 374. The details of the suit are not clear.

³ Amesbury, which the Queensberrys acquired in 1724, dates back to the tenth century when Queen Alfrida founded a Benedictine nunnery there. The abbey was razed in the mid sixteenth century and the modern Amesbury built on its ruins in 1661 by John Webb, son-in-law of Inigo Jones. During the Queensberrys' tenure, two wings were added, which are believed to have been designed by the Earl of Burlington. See *The Victoria History of the Counties of England*, vol. iii, *A History of Wiltshire*, eds. R. B. Pugh and Elizabeth Crittall (1956), pp. 242–59.

70. Gay *to* Swift 27 *April 1731*

Add. 4806

Amesbury April 27. 1731

Dear Sir. / Yours without a date I receiv'd two days after my return to this place from London where I stayd only four days. I saw Mr Pope who was much better, I din'd with him at Lord Oxford's who never fails drinking your health & is always very inquisitive after every thing that concerns you. Mr Pulteney had receiv'd your Letter & seem'd very much pleas'd with it, & I thought you very much too in the good graces of the Lady. Sir W Wyndham, who you will by this time have heard hath buried Lady Catherine was at Dawley in great Affliction. Dr Arbuthnot I found in good health & spirits; His neighbour Mr Lewis was gone to the Bath. Mrs Patty Blount I saw two or three times who will be very much pleas'd when she knows you so kindly remember her; I am afraid Mrs Howard will not be so well satisfied with the compliments you send her.[1] I breakfasted with her twice at Mrs Blounts, & she told me that her indisposition had prevented her answering your Letter; this she desir'd me to tell you & that she would write to you soon and she desires you will accept of her compliments in the mean time by me. You should consider circumstances before you censure; twill be too long for a Letter to make her Apology, but when I see you, I believe I shall convince you that you mistake her. The day before I left London I gave orders for buying two Southsea or India Bonds for you which carry four p Cent & are as easily turn'd into ready money as Bank Bills; which by this time I suppose is done. I shall go to London again for a few days in about a fortnight or three weeks, and then I will take care of the twelve pound affair with Mrs Lancelot as you direct; or if I hear of Mr Pope's being in town, I will do it sooner by a Letter to him. When I was in town (after a bashfull fit for having writ something like a Love Letter, & in two years not making one visit) I writ to Mrs Drelin-

---

[1] In a letter to Mrs. Howard dated 21 November 1730 Swift, who distrusted Mrs. Howard, accused her of acting as a 'Courtier' and not as a friend concerning his and Gay's interests at Court. See *Swift Corr.* iii. 422–5.

court to Apologize for my behaviour, & receiv'd a civil Answer but had not time to see her;[1] they are naturally very civil so that I am not so sanguine to interpret this as any encouragement. I find by Mrs Barber that she very much interests herself in her Affair,[2] and indeed from every body who knows her she answers the character you first gave me. Whenever you come to England if you will put that confidence in me to give me notice I will meet you at your Landing place & conduct you hither, you have experience of me as a traveller, & I promise you I will not drop you upon the road for any visit whatever. You tell me of thanks that I have not given; I dont know what to say to people who will be perpetually laying one under obligations; my behaviour to you shall convince you that I am very sensible of 'em though I never once mention 'em. I look upon you as my best friend & counsellor. I long for the time when we shall meet & converse together; I will draw you into no great company besides those I live with, in short, if you insist upon it I will give up all great company for yours. These are conditions that I can hardly think you will insist upon after your declarations to the Dutchess who is more & more impatient to see you, & all my fear is that you will give up me for her which after my ungallant declaration would be very ungenerous. But we will settle this matter together when you come to Amesbury. After all I find I have been saying nothing; for, sp[ea]king of her, I am talking as if I were in my own power[.] You us'd to blame me for over-solicitude about myself, I am now grown so rich that I dont think myself worth thinking on, so that I will promise you never to mention myself or my own Affairs; but you ow'd it all to the inquisitiveness of your friendship; and ten to one but every now and then you will draw me in to talk of myself again. I sent you a gross state of my Fortune already. I have not room to draw it out in particulars. When you come over the Dutchess will state it to you. I have left no room for her to write, so that I will say nothing till my Letter is gone, but she would not forgive me if I did not send her compliments.

[1] See also Letter 62.

[2] i.e. Mrs. Drelincourt interested herself in Mrs. Barber's 'Affair' by subscribing for a volume of her poems.

Address: To / The Revd Dr Swift / Dean of St Patrick's / in Dublin /
Ireland / by way of London
Postmark: 28/AP
Endorsement: May. 4th. 1731 / Mr Gay / Answd. Jun. 29th / 1731
[Swift's hand]

71. Gay *to* Mrs. Howard *8 July 1731*

Add. 22626

Your Letter was not ill-bestow'd, for I found in it such an
air of satisfaction that I have a pleasure every time I think of
it. I fancy, (though by her Silence she seems to approve of
your Ladyship's[1] conduct) the Dutchess will meet you at
Highclear,[2] for those that have a real friendship cannot be
satisfied with general relations, they want to enquire into
the minute circumstances of life that they may be sure things
are as happy as they appear to be, and that is a curiosity that
is excuseable. I dont like Lawsuits, I wish you could have
your right without 'em,[3] for I fancy there never was one
since the world began, that besides the cost was not attended
with anxiety & vexation; but as you descended from Lawyers, what might be my plague perhaps may be only your
amusement. Nobody but yourself hath let us know any thing
about you, judge then how welcome your Ladyships Letter
was to me. I find this change of life of yours[4] is a subject that
I cannot so well write upon, 'tis a thing that one cannot so
well judge of in general, but as for your Ladyship's conduct
in this juncture my approbation goes for nothing for all the
world knows that I am partial. When you have a mind to
make me happy write to me, for of late I have had but very
little chance, & only chance, of seeing you. If ever you
thought well of me; if ever you believ'd I wish'd you well, &

[1] Mrs. Howard was now Countess of
Suffolk by virtue of her estranged husband's succession to the earldom. Thus,
Gay addresses her as 'your Ladyship',
for which he was roundly berated by the
new Countess in an ensuing letter.

[2] Highclere, in Hampshire, estate of
the Hon. Robert Sawyer Herbert, was

about twenty miles from Amesbury.

[3] The late Earl of Suffolk had made
some bequests to Mrs. Howard which
her husband was contesting. See Lady
Suffolk to Gay, 29 June 1731, *Suffolk
Corr.* ii. 2.

[4] i.e. her new title and new position as
Mistress of the Robes to Queen Caroline.

wish'd to be of service to you think the same of me, for I am
the same & shall always be so.

Mr Pope I fear is determin'd never to write / to me. I hope
he is well. if you see Mrs Blount / or Mr Pope I beg 'em to
accept my compliments.

July 8. 1731.

72. Gay *and the* Duchess of Queensberry *to* Swift
18 July 1731

Add. 4806

                              Jully thee Eighteenth / 1731
[DUCHESS] you are my Dear freind I am sure, for you are
hard to be found, that you are so is certainly owing to some
Evil genius, for if you say true this is the very properest
place you can repair to, there is not a Head here upon any of
our Shoulders that is not att some times worse than yours
can posible be att your worst[1] & not one to compare with
yours when at best (except your friends are your sworn
Lyars) so in one respect at least you'll find things just as they
could be wishd tis farther necessary to assure you that the
Dutchess is nei[ther] young or healthy. she lives in all the
Spirits that she can and with as little grandeur as she can
posibly, she too as well as you, can scold & command, but
she can be silent, & obey, if she pleases—& then for a good
Nurse tis out of dispute that she must prove an excelent one,
who has been so experienc'd in the infirmitys of others & off
her own. as for talking nonsence provided you do it on purpose s[he] has no objection, there's some sence in nonsense
when it does not come by Chance. in short I am very sure
that she has sett her Heart upon seeing you att this place,
here are women enough to attend you, if you should happen
not to approve of her. she has not one fine Lady belonging to
her, or her house. she is impatient to be govern'd, & is chear-
fully determin'd that you shall quietly injoy your own will &
pleasure as long as ever you please. [GAY] You shall ride, you
shall walk, & she will be glad to follow your example; and
this will be doing good at the same time to her & your self.

        [1] Referring to Swift's attacks of 'giddiness'.

I had not heard from you so long that I was in fears about you & in the utmost impatience for a Letter. I had flatter'd myself your Lawsuit was at an end & that your own money was in your own pockets, & about a month ago I was every day expecting a summons to Bristol.[1] Your Money is either getting or losing something for I have plac'd it in the funds, for I am grown so much a man of business, that is to say so covetous, that I cannot bear to let a Summ of money lye idle. Your friend Mrs H. is now Countess of Suffolk; I am still so much a dupe that I think you mistake her. Come to Amesbury & you & I will dispute this matter & the Dutchess shall be judge[.] But I fancy you will object against her, for I will be so fair to you as to own that I think she is of my side. But in short you shall chuse any impartial referee you please. I have heard from her, Mr Pope hath seen her, I [be]g that you would suspend your judgment 'till we talk over this affair together; for I fancy by your Letter you have neither heard from her or seen her, so that you cannot at present be as good a judge as we are. I'll be a Dupe for you at any time, therefore I beg it of you that you would let me be a Dupe in quiet.

As you have had several attacks of the giddiness you at present complain of, & that it hath formerly left you, I will hope that at this instant you are perfectly well; though my fears were so very great before I receiv'd your Letter that I may probably flatter myself & think you better than you are. As to my being a Manager for the Duke you have been misinform'd. Upon the discharge of an unjust Steward, he took the Administration into his own hands; I own I was call'd in to his assistance when the state of affairs was in the greatest confusion; Like an Ancient Roman I came put[ti]ng helping hand to set Affairs right, and as soon as it was done, I am retir'd again as a private man. [DUCHESS] what you imagin'd you heard her[2] say was a good deall in her Stile, t'was a thousand to one she had said so, but I must do her the justice to say that she did not either in thought or word; I am sure she wants to be better acquainted with you for which she has found out ten thousand reasons that we'll tell

---

1 To meet Swift on his arrival from Ireland and conduct him to Amesbury.
2 Mrs. Howard.

you if you'll come. [GAY] By your Letter I cannot guess
whether we are like to see you or no. Why might not the
Amesbury Downs make you better? [DUCHESS] Dear Sir Mr
Gay tells me I must write on upon his line for fear of taking
[up?] too much room. T'was his fault that I omitted my
Duty in his last letter, for he never told me one word of
writing to you till he had sent a way his letter, however as a
mark of my great humility, I shall be ready & glad to aske
your pardon upon my knees as soon as ever you come, tho
not in fault. I own this is a little mean spirited, which I hope
will not make a bad impression, considering you are the
occation. I submit to all your conditions, so pray come, for
I have not only promis'd my self, but Mr Gay also the Satisfaction to hear you talk as much nonsense as you can possibly
utter. [GAY] You will read in the Gazette of a friend of yours
who hath lately had the dignity of being disgrac'd;¹ for he &
every body (except five or six) look upon it in the same light.
I know, were you here, you would congratulate him upon it.
I payd the twelve pounds to Mrs Lancelot for the uses you
directed. I have no Scheme at present either to raise my fame
or fortune; I daily reproach myself for my idleness; you know
one cannot write when one will; I think and I reject; one day
or other perhaps I may think on something that may engage
me to write. You and I are alike in one particular, (I wish to
be so in many) I mean that we hate to write upon other folk's
Hints. I love to have my own Scheme and to treat it in my
own way; this perhaps may be taking too much upon myself, & I may make a bad choice, but I find I can always
enter into a Scheme of my own with more ease & pleasure
than into that of any other Body. I long to see you; I long to
hear from you; I wish you health, I wish you happiness; &
I [sho]uld be very happy myself to be witness that you
[Sentence incomplete]

Address: To / The Reverend Dr Swift / Dean of St Patrick's / in
  Dublin / Ireland / by way of London
Postmark: 19/IY
Endorsement: Rx Jul. 25th 1731 / Mr Gay, and / Du——s of Qu——
  [Swift's hand]

---

¹ Pulteney, who had been removed from the list of Privy Councillors.

73. Gay *and the* Duke of Queensberry *to* Swift[1]
[*1 November 1731*]

Add. 4806

[GAY] For about this month or six weeks past, I have been rambling from home; or have been at what I may not improperly call other homes, at Dawley & at Twickenham; & I really think at every one of my homes you have as good a pretension as myself, for I find 'em all exceedingly disappointed by the Lawsuit that hath kept you this summer from us. Mr Pope told me that Affair was now over, that you have the Estate that was your security, I wish you had your own money, for I wish you free from every Engagement that keeps us one from another. I think you decypher'd the last Letter we sent you very judiciously.[2] You may make your own conditions at Amesbury where I am at present, you may do the same at Dawley, and Twickenham you know is your own; But if you rather chuse to live with me, (that is to say, if you will give up your right & title) I will purchase the house you & I us'd to dispute about over-against Ham walks on purpose to entertain you.[3] name your day & it shall be done. I have liv'd with you, & I wish to do so again in any place & upon any terms. The Dutchess does not know of my writing, but I promis'd to acquaint the Duke the next time

---

[1] Dated as to month and day from the postmark. The year is established by Swift's endorsement.

[2] See the joint letter of 18 July wherein Gay and the Duchess alternate at will in writing. Swift's deciphering task was not excessively demanding. The two hands are quite distinct and the Duchess's spelling and syntax are unique.

[3] Apparently not the 'widow's house' which Gay talked of buying earlier (see Letters 53, 61). A remark in Swift's reply indicates that the house 'over-against Ham walks' belonged to Mrs. Howard. See *Swift Corr.* iii. 506. It is unlikely that Gay ever purchased either of these properties, although a tradition

of 'Gay's house' at Marble Hill has persisted. Cobbett (*Memorials of Twickenham*, p. 243) asserted that 'Gay probably had a house at Marble Hill as well as on the other side of the river with the Duke of Queensberry'; and an article, 'Tales of the Thames', by Arthur M. Young in the *Local Illustrated News* (Boroughs of Richmond and Twickenham) for 29 December 1923 carried an illustration with the caption, 'Gay's House—Author of the Beggars' Opera —(an annexe of Marble Hall), which has been pulled down'. The basis for the tradition was probably an apartment made available to Gay when he visited Marble Hill, which, in time, was expanded to 'Gay's house'.

I writ to you, & for aught I know [he] may tell the Dutchess, & she may tell Sir W. Wyndham, who is now here, & for fear they should all have something to say to you I leave the rest of the paper 'till I see the Duke.

[DUKE] Mr Gay tells me you seem to doubt what authority my Wife & he have to invite a person hither who by agreement is to have the government of the place during his stay, when at the same time it does not appear that the present master of these Demesnes hath been consulted in it. The truth of the matter is this, I did not know whether you might not have suspected me for a sort of a pert coxcomb had I put in my word in the late correspondance between you & my Wife. Ladies (by the Courtesie of the World) enjoy priviledges not allow'd to men & in many cases the same thing is call'd a favour from a Lady which might perhaps be look'd upon as impertinence from a man. Upon this reflection I have hitherto refrain'd from writing to you having never had the pleasure of conversing with you otherways & as that is a thing I most sincerely wish I would not venture to meddle in a negotiation that seem'd to be in so fair a way of producing that desirable end; but our friend John has not done me justice if he has never mention'd to you how much I wish for the pleasure of seeing you here & tho I have not till now avowedly taken any steps towards bringing it about, what has pass'd conducive to it has been all along with my privity & consent & I do now formally ratify all the preliminary articles & conditions agreed to on the part of my Wife & will undertake for the due observance of them. I depend upon my friend John to answer for my sincerity; I was not long at Court & have been a Country gentleman for some time.

> Poll manu sub linus darque dds
> Sive Nig tig gnipite gnaros[1]

Address: To the Revd: Doctor Swift / Dean of St: Patrick's / in Dublin / Ireland
Postmark: 1/NO
Endorsement: Mr Gay and the / Duke of Queensberry / No date / Rx Novr. 8th. 1731 [Swift's hand]

[1] The two lines of gibberish were added by the Duchess. For their origin and possible significance, see *Notes and Queries*, 198 (1953), 160–1.

74. Gay *and* Pope *to* Swift *1 December 1731*

1740 (*Letters of Pope and Swift*)

December 1, 1731.

You us'd to complain that Mr. Pope and I would not let you speak: you may now be even with me, and take it out in writing. If you don't send to me now and then, the post-office will think me of no consequence, for I have no correspondent but you. You may keep as far from us as you please, you cannot be forgotten by those who ever knew you, and therefore please me by sometimes shewing that I am not forgot by you. I have nothing to take me off from my friendship to you; I seek no new acquaintance, and court no favour; I spend no shillings in coaches or chairs to levees or great visits, and as I don't want the assistance of some that I formerly convers'd with, I will not so much as seem to seek to be a dependant. As to my studies, I have not been entirely idle, though I cannot say that I have yet perfected any thing. What I have done is something in the way of those fables I have already publish'd.[1] All the money I get is by saving, so that by habit there may be some hopes (if I grow richer) of my becoming a miser. All misers have their excuses; The motive to my parsimony is independance. If I were to be represented by the Dutchess (she is such a downright niggard for me) this character might not be allow'd me; but I really think I am covetous enough for any who lives at the court-end of the town, and who is as poor as myself: for I don't pretend that I am equally saving with S——k.[2] Mr. Lewis desir'd you might be told that he hath five pounds of yours in his hands which he fancies you may have forgot, for he will hardly allow that a Verse-man can have a just knowledge of his own affairs. When you got rid of your law-suit, I was in hopes you had got your own, and was free from every vexation of the law: but Mr. Pope tells me you are not entirely out of your perplexity, though you have the security

---

[1] The second volume of the *Fables* was not published until 29 September 1738, six years after Gay's death.

[2] Charles Douglas, 2nd Earl of Selkirk, who appears in Pope's *Epistle to Bathurst* as the miser, Harpax (ll. 93–94).

now in your own possession; but still your case is not so bad
as Captain Gulliver's, who was ruin'd by having a decree for
him with costs. I have had an injunction for me against
pyrating-booksellers,[1] which I am sure to get nothing by,
and will, I fear, in the end drain me of some mony. When I
begun this prosecution, I fancy'd there would be some end
of it, but the law still goes on, and 'tis probable I shall some
time or other see an Attorney's bill as long as the Book. Poor
Duke Disney is dead, and hath left what he had among
his friends, among whom are Lord Bolingbroke 500 l. Sir
William Wyndham's youngest son, 500 l. Gen Hill, 500 l.
Lord Massam's son 500 l.

You have the good wishes of those I converse with, they
know they gratify me when they remember you; but I really
think they do it purely for your own sake. I am satisfied with
the love and friendship of good men, and envy not the de-
merits of those who are more conspicuously distinguish'd.
Therefore as I set a just value upon your friendship, you
cannot please me more than letting me now and then know
you remember me (the only satisfaction of distant friends!)

P.S. Mr. Gay's is a good letter, mine will be a very dull
one; and yet what you will think the worst of it is what should
be its excuse, that I write in a head-ach that has lasted three
days. I am never ill but I think of your ailments, and repine
that they mutually hinder our being together: tho' in one
point I am apt to differ from you, for you shun your friends
when you are in those circumstances, and I desire them; your
way is the more generous, mine the more tender. Lady ——
took your letter very kindly,[2] for I had prepared her to
expect no answer under a twelve-month; but kindness perhaps is a word not applicable to courtiers. However she is an
extraordinary woman there, who will do you common justice.
For God's sake why all this scruple about Lord B——'s[3]
keeping your horses who has a park, or about my keeping
you on a pint of wine a day? We are infinitely richer than you
imagine; John Gay shall help me to entertain you, tho' you

---

[1] To prohibit unauthorized editions
of *Polly*. See Arbuthnot to Swift, 9 June
1729, *Swift Corr.* iii. 338; see also
Favorite, p. 275.

[2] Lady Suffolk (Mrs. Howard) to
whom Swift wrote a lengthy letter on
16 October 1731. See *Swift Corr.* iii.
499–502.   [3] Bolingbroke.

come like King Lear with fifty knights—Tho' such prospects as I wish,[1] cannot now be formed for fixing you with
us, time may provide better before you part again: the old
Lord may die, the benefice may drop, or at worst, you may
carry me into Ireland. You will see a word of Lord B——'s
and one of mine;[2] which with a just neglect of the present
age, consult only posterity; and with a noble scorn of politicks, aspire to philosophy. I am glad you resolve to meddle
no more with the low concerns and interests of parties, even
of countries (for countries are but larger parties) *Quid verum
atque decens, curare, & rogare, nostrum sit.*[3] I am much
pleased with your design upon Rochefoucault's maxim,[4]
pray finish it. I am happy whenever you join our names
together: so would Dr. Arbuthnot be, but at this time can
be pleas'd with nothing; for his darling son is dying in all
probability, by the melancholy account I received this
morning.

The paper you ask me about is of little value.[5] It might have
been a seasonable satire upon the scandalous language and
passion with which men of condition have stooped to treat
one another: surely they sacrifice too much to the people,
when they sacrifice their own characters, families, &c. to the
diversion of that rabble of readers. I agree with you in my
contempt of most popularity, fame, &c. even as a writer I
am cool in it, and whenever you see what I am now writing,
you'll be convinced I would please but a few, and (if I could)
make mankind less Admirers, and greater Reasoners. I study
much more to render my own portion of being easy, and to
keep this peevish frame of the human body in good humour.
Infirmities have not quite unmann'd me, and it will delight
you to hear they are not increas'd, tho' not diminish'd. I
thank God I do not very much want people to attend me,
tho' my Mother now cannot. When I am sick I lie down,

---

[1] Listed below—the death of Bolingbroke's aged father; a benefice for Swift
at Bolingbroke's disposal—which events
would enable Swift to return to England.

[2] Bolingbroke's 'Essays Addressed to
Mr. Pope' and Pope's *Essay on Man.*

[3] Horace, *Epistles*, I. i. 11.

[4] 'Verses on the Death of Dr. Swift'
which, according to Swift's sub-title, is

based on one of La Rochefoucauld's
maxims.

[5] As Sherburn suggested, the reference is most likely to Arbuthnot's *Brief
Account of Mr. John Ginglicutt's Treatise
concerning the Altercation or Scolding of
the Ancients* (1731), which may have
been under consideration for the *Miscel-
lanies* of 1732.

when I am better I rise up: I am used to the head-ach, &c.
If greater pains arrive (such as my late rheumatism) the
servants bathe and plaster me, or the surgeon scarifies me,
and I bear it, because I must. This is the evil of Nature, not
of Fortune. I am just now as well as when you was here: I
pray God you were no worse. I sincerely wish my life were
past near you, and such as it is I would not repine at it.—All
you mention remember you, and wish you here.

75. Gay *to* Swift *18 January 1731/2*

Add. 4806

Dear Sir. / It is now past nine a clock, I deferr'd sitting
down to write to you in expectation to have seen Mr Pope
who left me two or three hours ago to try to find Lord
Burlington, within whose walls I have not been admitted
this year & a half but for what reason I know not.[1] Mr Pope
is just this minute come in, but had not the good luck to find
him, so that I cannot give you any satisfaction in the Affair
you writ last about.[2] He designs to see him to morrow, & if
any thing can be done he says you shall hear from him.

By the beginning of my Letter you see how I decline in
favour, but I look upon it as my particular distinction, that
as soon as the Court gains a man I lose him; tis a mortification I have been us'd to, so I bear it as a Philosopher should.

The Letter which you writ to me & the Duke I receiv'd,
& Mr Pope show'd me that directed to him, which gave me
more pleasure than all the Letters you have writ since I saw
you as it give me hopes of seeing you soon.

Were I to acquaint the Duke & Dutchess of my writing
I know that they would have something to say to you &
perhaps would prevent my sending the Letter this post, so
I chuse to say nothing about it. You are in great favour &
esteem with all those that love me, which is one great reason
that I love & esteem them.

---

[1] Perhaps because of his defection to
the Queensberrys. Or perhaps because
of his controversial position at Court,
which, as Gay hints below, Burlington
was now cultivating.

[2] The repair of the monument to
Burlington's ancestor, the 1st Earl of
Cork, in St. Patrick's, Dublin. See
Swift to Gay, 20 November 1729, *Swift
Corr.* iii. 361.

Whenever you will order me to turn your fortune into ready money, I will obey you; but I chuse to leave it where it is 'till you want it, as it carrys some interest. Though it might be now sold to some advantage, & is liable to rises & falls with the other stocks it may be higher as well as lower; so I will not dispose of it 'till I hear from you. I am impatient to see you so are all your friends. You have taken your resolution, & I shall henceforth every week expect an agreeable surprise. The Bellman rings for the Letter so I can say no more.

London. / Jan. 18. 1731/2.

Address: To / The Reverend Dr Swift / Dean of St Patrick's in / Dublin. / Ireland.
Postmark: 18/IA
Endorsement: Mr Gay. / Janr. 18th. 1731–2 / Answred. [Swift's hand]

76. Gay *to Swift*[1] [*13 March 1731/2*]

Add. 4806

Dear Sir. / I hope this unlucky accident of hurting your Leg will not prevent your coming to us this Spring though you say nothing about it; All your friends expect it, & particularly my Landlord & Landlady, who are my friends as much as ever, & I should not think 'em so, if they were not as much yours. The Downs of Amesbury are so smooth that neither horse nor man can hardly make a wrong step, so that you may take your exercise with us with greater security. If you can prevail with the Dutchess to ride & walk with you, you will do her good, but that is a motive I could never prevail with her to comply with. I wish you would try whether your oratory could get over this difficulty. General Dormer, Sir Clement Cotterel & I set out to morrow morning for Rousham[2] in Oxfordshire to stay ten days or a fortnight. The Dutchess will undertake to recommend the Lords of her acquaintance to attend Mr Reeves his Cause[3] if it

---

[1] Dated from internal evidence (Gay's remark, 'to morrow being the 14th of March') and Swift's endorsement.

[2] The ancestral seat of the Cottrell-

Dormer family, twelve miles north of Oxford. See F. G. Brabant, *Oxfordshire* (1933), pp. 223 ff.

[3] A suit involving William Ryves,

should come on before our return; the Duke will do the same. Her Grace too hath undertaken to answer your Letter. I have not dispos'd of your S. Sea Bonds; There is a years interest due at Lady day. But if I were to dispose of 'em at present I should lose a great deal of the premium I pay'd for 'em; perhaps they may fall lower, but I cannot prevail with myself to sell 'em. The Roguerys that have been discover'd in some other companys I beleive makes 'em all have less credit. I find myself dispirited for want of having some pursuit; indolence & idleness are the most tiresome things in the world, & I begin to find a dislike to society. I think I ought to try to break myself of it, but I cannot resolve to set about it. I have left of almost all my great acquaintance, which saves me something in Chair-hire, though in that article the town is still very expensive. Those who were your old acquaintance are almost the only people I now visit, and indeed upon trying all I like 'em best. Lord Cornbury refus'd the Pension that was offer'd him.[1] He is chosen to represent the University of Oxford, (in the room of Mr Bromley) without opposition. I know him and I think he deserves it. He is a Young Nobleman of learning & Morals which is so particular that I know you will respect & value him, & to my great comfort he lives with us in our family. Mr Pope is in town & in good health I lately past a week with him at Twickenham. I must leave the rest to the Dutchess for I must pack up my shirts to set out to morrow being the 14th of March the day after I receiv'd your Letter. If you would advise the Dutchess to confine me four hours a day to my own room while I am in the country I will write; for I cannot confine myself as I ought.

Address: [In another hand] To / The Revd. Dr. Swift / Dean of St. Patricks / in / Dublin.
Postmark: 8/AP²
Frank: Cornbury / free.
Endorsement: Mr Gay Apr. 13th / 1732 / Answd. May. 6th. 1732. [Swift's hand]

nephew of Swift's old friend, Jerome Ryves, one-time Dean of St. Patrick's. The case had resulted in an appeal to the House of Lords.

   [1] For one version of Cornbury's

refusal of the pension, see Spence, *Anecdotes*, p. 292.

   ² The discrepancy between the date of writing and the date of posting can be resolved as follows: Gay began the letter

77. Gay *to* Swift *16 May 1732*

Add. 4806

London May 16. 1732.

Dear Sir. / To morrow we set out for Amesbury where I propose to follow your advice of employing myself about some work against next winter. You seem'd not to approve of my writing more Fables; those I am now writing have a prefatory discourse before each of 'em by way of Epistle, & the Morals of most of 'em are of the political kind; which makes 'em run into a greater length than those I have already publish'd. I have already finish'd about fifteen or sixteen; four or five more would make a volume of the same size as that first. Though this is a kind of writing that appears very easy, I find it the most difficult of any that I ever undertook; after I have invented one Fable, and finish'd it, I despair of finding out another, But I have a moral or two more which I wish to write upon. I have also a sort of a Scheme to raise my finances by doing something for the Stage;[1] with this & some reading & a great deal of exercise I propose to pass my summer; I am sorry it must be without you. Why can't you come, & saunter about upon the Downs a Horseback in the Autumn to mark the partridges for me to shoot for your dinner? Yesterday I receiv'd your Letter, & notwithstanding your reproaches of Laziness I was four or five hours about business & did not spend a shilling in a Coach or a Chair. I receiv'd a years interest on your two Bonds which is Eight pounds. I have four of my own; I have deposited all of 'em in the hands of Mr Hoare to receive the half year's interest at Michaelmas. The Premium of the Bonds is fallen a great deal since I bought yours; I gave very near six pounds on each bond, and they are now sold for about fifty shillings. Every thing is very precarious, & I have no opinion of any of their publick Securitys, but I do not know what to do with

on 13 March and left space for the Duchess to write. The following morning he set out for Rousham, assuming that the Duchess would finish and post the letter. The Duchess, however, was suddenly called to Winchester School by the illness of her son, Lord Drumlanrig

(see Letter 77). The neglected letter was finally franked and posted on 8 April by Lord Cornbury.

[1] The opera, *Achilles*, produced at the Theatre Royal, Lincoln's Inn Fields, on 10 February 1733, after Gay's death.

our money. I believe the Parliament next year intend to examine the Southsea Scheme. I do not know whether it will be prudent to trust our money there till that time. I did what I could to assist Mr Ryves, & I am very glad that he hath found Justice. Lord Bathurst spoke for him & was very zealous in bringing on his Cause. The Dutchess intended to write in my last Letter, but she set out all on a sudden to take care of Lord Drumlanrig, who was taken ill of the Small pox at Winchester School. He is now perfectly well recover'd, (for he had a favourable kind) to the great joy of our family. I think she ought, as she intends to renew her correspondance with you at Amesbury. I was at Dawley on Sunday, Lady B—— continues in a very bad state of health, but still retains her Spirits; You are always rememberd there with great respect & friendship. Mrs Pope is so worn out with Old Age, but without any distemper, that I look upon her Life as very uncertain; Mr Pope's state of health is much in the same way as when you left him. as for myself, I am often troubled with the Cholick, I have as much inattention, & have, I think lower Spirits than usual, which I impute to my having no one pursuit in life. I have many compliments to make you from the Duke & Dutchess, & Lord Bolingbroke, Bathurst, Sir W. Wyndham, Mr Pulteney, Dr Arbuthnot, Mr Lewis &c. Every one of 'em is disappointed in your not coming among us. I have not seen Dean Berkeley, but have read his Book, & like many parts of it, but in general think with you, that it is too Speculative, at least for me.[1] Dr Delany I have very seldom seen; he did not do me the honour to advise with me about any thing he hath publish'd; I like your thoughts upon these sort of writings and I should have advis'd him as you did, though I had lost his good opinion. I write in very great haste; for I have many things to do before I go out of town. Pray, make me as happy as you can, & let me hear from you often; But I am still in hopes to see you; & will expect a summons one day or other to come to Bristol, in order to be your Guide to Amesbury.

Endorsement: Rx Jun. 10th. 1732 / Mr Gay, by Mr / Reeves / Ansd. Jul. 10th. 1732. [Swift's hand]

[1] Berkeley's *Alciphron, or The Minute Philosopher* would scarcely appeal to a reader of *Les Contes Tartares*.

78. Gay *and the* Duchess of Queensberry *to* Swift
24 July 1732

Add. 4806

[DUCHESS] Ambresbury Jully the 24th: / 1732.

[GAY] Dear Sir. / As the circumstances of our money affairs are alter'd I think myself oblig'd to acquaint you with 'em as soon as I can which if I had not receiv'd your Letter last post I should have done now. I left your two S. Sea Bonds, and four of my own in Mr Hoare's hands when I came out of town that he might receive the interest for us when due, or if you should want your money that you might receive it upon your order. Since I came out of town, the Southsea Company have come to a resolution to pay off 50 p Cent of their Bonds with the interest on the 50 p Cent to Michaelmas next. so that there is now half of our fortunes in Mr Hoare's hands at present without any interest going on. As you seem to be inclin'd to have your money remitted to Ireland I will not lay out the summ that is paid into his hands in any other thing till I have your orders. I cannot tell what to do with my own; I believe I shall see Mr Hoare in this country very soon, for he hath a house not above six miles from us,[1] & intend to advise with him, though in the present situation of affairs I expect to be left to take my own way. The remaining 50 p Cent, were it to be sold at present bears a premium, but the premium on the 50 that was paid in is sunk. I do not know whether I write intelligibly to you upon this subject. I cannot send you the particulars of your account, though I know I am in debt to you for interest besides your principal, & you will understand so much of what I intend to inform you that half of your money is now in Mr Hoare's hands without any interest so since I cannot send you the particulars of your account I will now say no more about it. I shall finish the work I intended this summer, but I look upon the success in every respect to be precarious. You judge very rightly of my present situation that I cannot

---

[1] At Stourhead, which was nearer thirty than six miles from Amesbury. See John Ogilby, *Brittania Depicta*, 4th ed. (1731), pp. 78, 134.

propose to succeed by favour, & I don't think, if I could flatter myself that I had any degree of merit much cou'd be expected from that unfashionable pretension. I have almost done every thing I propos'd in the way of Fables, but not set the last hand to them; though they will not amount to half the number, I believe they will make much such another volume as the last. I find it the most difficult task I ever undertook, but I have determin'd to go through with it, and after this, I believe I shall never have courage enough to think any more in this way. Last Post I had a Letter from Mr Pope who informs me he hath heard from you, and that he is preparing some scatter'd things of yours & his for the Press;[1] I believe I shall not see him 'till the Winter, for by riding & walking I am endeavouring to lay in a stock of health to squander in town; You see in this respect my scheme is very like the Country Gentlemen in regard to their revenues. As to my eating & drinking I live as when you knew me, so that in that point we shall agree very well in living together; and the Dutchess will answer for me that I am cur'd of inattention, for I never forget any thing she says to me. [DUCHESS] for he never hears what I say so cannot forget. if I served him the same way I should not care a farthing ever to be better acquainted with my Tunbridg acquaintance;[2] which by my attention to him I have learnt to sett my heart upon I began to give over all hopes & from thence began my neglect. I think this is a very good philosophical reason, tho there might be annother given; when fine Ladys are in London tis very genteel & allowable to forgit their best freinds, which if I thought modestly of myself, must needs be you, because you know little of me. till you do more pray dont perswaid Mr: Gay that he is discreet enough to live alone; for I do assure you he is not, or I either[.] we are of great use to one another for we never flatter or contradict but when tis absolutely necessary & then we do to some purpose particularly the first agree's mightily with our constitutions. if ever we quarrell twill be about a peice of Bread & butter for some body is never sick except he eates too much of it. he will not quarrell with y[ou] for a Glass or so for by that means he hopes to be able in time to Gulp down some of those fourty millions of Schemes that hindred him from being good company.[1] I would fain see you here, there is so fair a Chance that one of us must be pleasd, perhaps both, you with an old acquaintance & I with a new one. tis so well worth taking a jurney for, that if the Mountain will not come to Mahomet Mahomet must come to the Mountain, but before either of our journeys are settled I desire you would resolve me one question—whether a man who thinks himself well where he is, should look out for his house & Servants before tis convenient, before he grows old, or before a person with whom he lives) pulls him by the Sleeve in private (according to oath) & tells him they have enough of his Company.[2] he will not let me write one word more but that I have very great regard for you &cc the Duke is very much yours & will never leave you to your wine. many thanks for Drum I wish to receive your congratulations for the other Boy you may beleive.[3]

Address: For / the Revd: Dr: Swift Dean of St: Patricks / in Dublin / Ireland / by way / of London
Postmark: 26/[indistinct]
Endorsement: Mr Gay & Du——s of Qu——ry. / Rx Aug. 1st / 1732 [Swift's hand]

79. Gay *and the* Duchess of Queensberry *to* Swift
28 *August* 1732

Add. 4806

Amesbury. Aug. 28. 1732.

Dear Sir / Mr Hoare hath a hundred and odd pounds of yours in his hands, which you may have whenever you will please to draw upon me for it; I know I am more indebted

---

[1] See Gay's protestation that he was unable to write without the inspiration of wine (Letter 59). See also Letter 69.
[2] Gay had evidently mentioned his scheme of buying a house in Twicken-

ham to the Duchess. See also Letter 73 and footnote.
[3] Apparently the Queensberrys' other son, Lord Charles, had also contracted smallpox.

to you (I mean besides the Southsea Bond of a hundred that still subsists) but I cannot tell you exactly how your account stands 'till I come to town. I have money of my own too in Mr Hoare's hands which I know not at present how to dispose of; I believe I shall leave it without interest till I come to town, & shall then be at the same loss how to dispose of it as now. I have an intention to get more money next Winter but am prepard for disappointments which I think it is very likely I shall meet with yet as you think it convenient & necessary that I shou'd have more than I have you see I resolve to do what I can to oblige you. If my designs should not take effect I desire you will be as easy under it as I shall be, for I find you so solicitous about me that you cannot bear my [dis]appointments as well as I can. If I dont write intelligibly to you, ['tis] because I wou'd not have the Clerkes of the Post office know every thing I am doing. If you would have come here this summer you might with me have help'd to have drunk up the Duke's Wine and sav'd your money. I am grown so saving of late, that I very often reproach myself with being covetous, and I am very often afraid that I shall have the trouble of having money & never have the pleasure of making use of it. I wish you could live among us, but not unless it could be to your ease & satisfaction. You insist upon your being Minister of Amesbury, Dawley, Twickenham, Riskings[1] & prebendary of Westminster; for your being Minister in those places I cannot promise you, but I know you might have a good living [in] every one of them. Gambadoes I have rid in,[2] and I think 'em a very fine and usefull invention, but I have not made use of 'em since I left Devonshire. I ride and walk every day to such excess that I am afraid I shall take a surfeit of it; I am sure, if I am not better in health after it, 'tis not worth the pains. I say this, though I have this season shot 19 brace of Partridges. I have very little acquaintance with our Vicar; he doth not live among us but resides at another Parish and I have not play'd at Back-Gammon with any body since I came to Amesbury

[1] Riskins (also Ritchings) Park, Bathurst's estate at Iver in Buckinghamshire.

[2] A long boot or legging attached to each side of the saddle to protect the rider's legs and feet from the weather. See *NED*. Swift had used them for riding while convalescing from his leg injury.

but Lady Harold and Lady Bateman. As Dr Delany hath taken away a fortune from us[1] I expect to be recommended in Ireland, if Godly Authors of Godly Books are intituled to such fortunes, I desire you would recommend me as a Moral one, I mean in Ireland, for that recommendation would not do in England. [DUCHESS] The Dutchess will not lend you two or three thousands pounds to keep up your dignity for reasons best known to Strada dal Poe,[2] but she had much rather give you that or ten thousand times more than to lay it out in a fine pettecoat to make her self respected. I beleive for all you give Mr. Gay such good advice that you are a very indiscreet person yourself, or elce you would come here to take care of your own affairs, & not be so indiscreet to send for your monies over to a place where there is none. Mr. Gay is a very rich man for I realy think he does not wish to be richer, but he will, for he is doing what you bid him, tho if it may not be allow'd he will acquire greater honour & less trouble, his Coveteousness at present is for health which he takes so much pains for that he does not allow himself time [to enjoy it?], neither does he allow himself time to be either absent or present. when he began to be a sportsman he had like to have killd a dog & now every day I expect he will kill himself, & then the Bread & butter affair can never be brought before you, it is realy an affair of too great consequence to be trusted [to] a letter. therefore pray come on purpose to deside it, if you do you will not hear how familiar I am with goody Dobson for I have seen goody Dobson play at that with so ill a grace, that I was determind never to risque any thing so unbecoming I am not beloved neither do I love any creature, except a very few) & those not for having any sort of merit but only because tis my humour, in this rank Mr. Gay stands first & yourself next if you like to

---

[1] Delany married a wealthy widow, Margaret Tenison, while in England. See *DNB* entry 'Delany'.

[2] A street (now Via Po) in the Court section of Turin. Filled with palaces and colonnaded for virtually the whole of its length, it was, in 1732, one of the finest streets in Europe. Sherburn suggested that it is used here as a symbol for banking interests. See *Pope Corr.* iii. 308,

n. 3. However, since the Earl of Essex, formerly the Duchess's brother-in-law, was then stationed in Turin as British Ambassador to the King of Sardinia (see *DNB* entry 'William Capell'; see also GEC, v. 146), there is room to speculate that this is an oblique reference to some unsatisfactory financial arrangement between the Queensberrys and the Earl.

be respected upon these conditions. now do you know me; he stands over me and scolds me for spelling ill & is very peevish (& sleepy) that I do not give him up the pen, for he has yawnd for it a thousand times, we both once heard a lady (who at that time we both thought well off)¹ wish that she had the best living in England to give you. it was not me, but I do wish it with all my heart, if Mr: Gay does not hang out false lights for his freind. [GAY] I had forgot to tell you that I very lately received a Letter from Twitenham in which was this paragraph. < Motte & another idle fellow I find have been writing to the Dean to get him to give them some Copyright which surely he will not be so indiscreet as to do when he knows my design (and has done these two months & more) surely I shou'd be a properer person to tru[st] the distribution of his works with than to a common Bookseller. here will be nothing but the ludicrous & h[umourou]s, none of the political or any things of consequence which are wholy at his own disposal; but at any rate it wou'd be silly in him to give a copy right to any which can only put the manner of publishing 'em hereafter out of his own & his friends power into that of Mercenarys.—I really think this a very usefull precaution considering how you have been treated by these sort of fellows.

The Duke is fast asleep or he wou'd add a line.

Address: To / the Revd / Dr Swift Dean / of St Patricks in / Dublin / Ireland / by way of London
Postmark: 30/AV
Endorsement: Rx. Sept. 5th. 1732 / Mr Gay, and / D——s of Qu——ry / Ansd. Oct. 10 1732 [Swift's hand]

80. Gay *to* Pope 7 *October 1732*

1737 (*Letters of Mr. Alexander Pope*)

Oct. 7, 1732.

I am at last return'd from my Somersetshire expedition,² but since my return I cannot so much boast of my health as

¹ The Queen.
² To visit Sir William Wyndham at Orchard Wyndham, as the text makes clear. Orchard Wyndham, near Williton, West Somerset, is still the home of the Wyndham family.

before I went, for I am frequently out of order with my colical complaints,[1] so as to make me uneasy and dispirited, though not to any violent degree. The reception we met with, and the little excursions we made were every way agreeable. I think the country abounds with beautiful prospects. Sir William Wyndham is at present amusing himself with some real improvements, and a great many visionary castles. We were often entertain'd with sea views and sea fish, and were at some places in the neighbourhood, among which I was mightily pleased with Dunster Castle near Minehead. It stands upon a great eminence, and hath a prospect of that town, with an extensive view of the Bristol Channel; in which are seen two small Islands, call'd the steep Holms and flat Holms, and on t'other side we could plainly distinguish the divisions of fields on the Welsh coast. All this journey I perform'd on horseback, and I am very much disappointed that at present I feel my self so little the better for it. I have indeed follow'd riding and exercise for three months successively, and really think I was as well without it, so that I begin to fear the illness I have so long and so often complain'd of is inherent in my constitution, and that I have nothing for it but patience.

As to your advice about writing Panegyrick,[2] 'tis what I have not frequently done. I have indeed done it sometimes against my judgment and inclination, and I heartily repent of it. And at present as I have no desire of reward, and see no just reason of praise, I think I had better let it alone. There are flatterers good enough to be found, and I wou'd not interfere in any Gentleman's profession. I have seen no verses upon these sublime occasions, so that I have no

[1] Arbuthnot attributed Gay's death on 4 December 1732 to 'an inflammation, and . . . at last a mortification of the bowels', and described it as 'the most precipitate case I ever knew' (Pope and Arbuthnot to Swift, 5 December 1732, *Pope Corr.* iii. 335). Although it is difficult to translate Arbuthnot's diagnosis into modern medical terms with any degree of certainty, a reasonable guess would be that Gay's final illness was some form of intestinal obstruction followed by peritonitis. Gay's recurring 'colical complaints' may well have been advance symptoms of the disorder.

[2] Pope had suggested that Gay write some verses on the Queen's Hermitage, the subterranean building which Caroline had built in the Royal Gardens at Richmond. See Pope to Gay, 2 October 1732, *Pope Corr.* iii. 318. On the Queen's Hermitage see Horace Walpole, *Reminiscences Written by Mr. Horace Walpole in 1788* (1924), p. 115.

emulation. Let the patrons enjoy the authors and the authors their patrons, for I know myself unworthy. / I am, &c.

81. Gay *to* Swift *16 November 1732*

Add. 4806

Novr. 16. 1732.

Dear Sir. / I am at last come to London before the family to follow my own inventions; in a week or fortnight I expect the family will follow me. You may now draw upon me for your money as soon as you please; I have some of my own too that lyes dead, and I protest I do not [know] which way at present to dispose of it; every thing is so very precarious. I paid Mrs Launcelot twelve pounds, and pay myself the five Guineas you had of me, and have deducted your Loss by paying off one of the Southsea bonds; and I find I have now remaining of yours two hundred and eleven pounds fifteen shillings and sixpence. And I believe over and above that summ there will be more owing to you upon account of interest on the Bonds about four or five pounds. Mr Hoare hath done this for me, but I have not had time to call upon him yet, so that I cannot be more particular. As the money now lyes in Mr Hoare's hands you see it is ready on demand; I believe you had best give notice when you draw on me for it, that I may not be out of the way. I have not as yet seen Mr Pope, but design in a day or two to go to him; though I am in hopes of seeing him here to day or to morrow. If my present project[1] succeeds you may expect a better account of my own fortune a little while after the holidays; but I promise myself nothing for I am determind that neither any body else or myself shall disappoint me. I wish the Arguments made use of to draw you here were every way of more consequence; I wou'd not have [you] change one comfort of life for another; I wish you to keep every one of those you have already with as many additional ones as you like. When sit down to consider on the choice of any subject to amuse

---

[1] The opera *Achilles*, which he had brought to London with him to arrange for its production. See Pope to Caryll, 14 December 1732, *Pope Corr.* iii. 337.

myself by writing, I find I have a natural propensity to write against Vice, so that I dont expect much encouragement, though I really think in justice I ought to be paid for stifling my inclinations, But the Great are ungratefull. Mr Pulteney's young son hath had the small Pox, and is perfectly recover'd; he is not in to[wn but]¹ is expected in about a week from the Bath. I must answer the Letter you wr[ote to the] Dutchess & me when her Grace comes to town, for I know she intended to have [writ some?] in it. Why can't you come among us in the beginning of the new Year? The C[ompany] will be then all in town and the Spring advancing upon us every day. What I me[an by the] Company is, those who call themselves your friends & I believe are so. 'Tis [believed?] the Parliament will not meet till about the middle of January. I have not been [idle] while I was in the Country, and I know your wishes in general & in particular that industry may always find it's account. Believe me, as I am, unchangeable in the regard, Love & esteem I have for you.

Address: To / The Revd. Dr Swift Dean / of St Patricks in / Dublin. / Ireland.

Endorsement: Mr Gay / Novr. 22. 1732 / He dyed soon after / His last Lettr [Swift's hand]

¹ There is a hole extending through the next seven lines of the manuscript.

APPENDIX[1]

Memorandum by Mr. Gay relative to the differences existing between Mrs. Howard and Mr. Howard

Add. 22626

Saturday 16 Decemr. 1727. I heard a Conversation Dr Arbuthnot being in the room with me to this effect.

A Person who said he was that day to dine with Mr H. came to Mrs H. & talk'd upon a proposal of Mr H & Lord Suffolk. Mrs H. told him that the Demands Mr H made were impossible to be comply'd with, & that she would not meddle in any thing that related to the Agreement of the Brothers about the Settlement of the Suffolk estate. The Person upon hearing this said, that he thought the matter was impracticable, but that he imagin'd Mr H's objection was to the Persons who were propos'd to be bound for the payment of the 1200 pounds a year to L[ord] Suffolk, as they were Peers, & could not be prosecuted by Law in case of Non performance. Mrs H reply'd that this objection might have been made to Lord Trevor,[2] to whom she had entirely referr'd her affairs, & that she would not, nor could not be perpetually sending a Peer upon her messages who was engag'd in publick business but that she left herself entirely to what he jud'gd reasonably for her to do, who had been her Guardian & was her near relation. He talk'd of settling the interest of four thousand pounds on her Son; this she absolutely refus'd by saying she had starv'd with Mr H, & would not put herself in a circumstance to starve without him. She said she wonder'd at Mr H's persisting in such unreasonable proposals when he had made the matter so publick, as to have advic'd with Lawyers belonging to all the Courts, & that in case of a Lawsuit she had reason & justice to make demands upon him.

[1] The two documents which follow appear out of sequence in the Suffolk Correspondence folio. Both are definitely in Gay's hand and, to the best of the editor's knowledge, both are published for the first time here. Gay's 'Memorandum' adds considerable detail to Hervey's account of the Howards' marital settlement, and, at the same time, clarifies Croker's somewhat cryptic reference to Arbuthnot's role in the proceedings (see *Suffolk Corr.* i. xv).

[2] Thomas Trevor, 1st Baron Trevor of Bromham, a distinguished jurist, then Lord Privy Seal.

She ended by desiring the Person not to report that she had made any offers or proposals she having referr'd this affair entirely to Lord Trevor.

Gay *to* 'Roger'[1]

Most Honour'd Roger / Though I am allow'd by every Different Sect to be a 'Timothy' Tim, yet in the person of your Grace I have a respect and esteem for a Roger; and under the Denomination I take this occasion to congratulate your coming to town. I hope by your Conversation with the Arbourers in the Country, you have acquir'd nothing of their manners but their cheerfull disposition. The Dutchess of Queensberry is here, and will not allow herself to be a Ralph, though she now & then has her Ralph Days. When your Grace comes here, you will not find any of the King's Chappell Women, for neither Viscount nor Lady William Paulet visit me in the morning. If you should meet a Rigadoon or two here of your acquaintance I hope it would not be disagreeable to you, for as now and then I see an Italian Woman I have some acquaintance with the Rigadoons. Every Body agrees Lady Jekyll is a Tim, the Dutchess of Queensberry is so too, how can you reconcile this? when I see you you shall know the names of your other Friends & Relations, for I look upon you as an ignorant Caxton Roger just come out of the Country.

P.S. / The Society of Tips are not allowd / to be of the Original Institution. / therefore I have not mention'd them.

[1] This curious document has resisted all efforts at explication. It is virtually undatable and there is no clue to the addressee. The reasonable supposition is Mrs. Howard, except that Gay, who was always punctilious about titles, twice uses the term 'your Grace'. The absence of heading, date, closing salutation, and address suggest that it may not have been a letter, in the strictest sense, but rather a personal note delivered by a servant or through a mutual friend.

The text has proved equally unproductive. The names, 'Roger', 'Timothy Tim', 'Ralph', obviously have special meaning but the editor has been unable to find the key to that meaning. Professor Emmett L. Avery has suggested that these names may have originated with some of the type characters in the drolls presented at Southwark and Bartholomew Fairs. Alternatively, Gay to 'Roger' may be a sample of the special slang developed by the Maids of Honour and the Ladies-in-Waiting, who were also fond of giving private nicknames to Court figures. See Lady Hervey to Mrs. Howard, 31 August 1728, *Suffolk Corr.* i. 320–1; Mrs. Howard to Lady Hervey, September [1728], ibid. i. 323. Gay, who was on the best of terms with the ladies of the Court, would, of course, be conversant with this patois.

INDEX

Addison, Joseph, 5 and n., 21, 22, 25, 39 n.

Aikman, William, painter, 74 n.

Alciphron, or The Minute Philosopher (Berkeley), 123 n.

Ambassador and his Functions, The (Abraham de Wicquefort), 15 and n.

Amesbury, Wilts., seat of the Duke of Queensberry, 41 n., 48 n., 52, 86, 93, 97 n., 100, 103, 104, 106, 107 and n., 109, 112, 113, 114, 120, 122, 123, 124 n., 127.

Amhurst, Nicholas, 22 n.

Amyand, Claude, 48 and n.

Amyand, Claudius, 48 n.

An Account of the State of the Roman Catholic Religion, 31 n.

'An Epitaph' (Prior), 91 and n.

An Explanation of the Paintings in the Royal Hospital at Greenwich (Thornhill), 53 n.

Arbuthnot, George, Dr. Arbuthnot's brother, 47, 71.

Arbuthnot, Dr. John, 7, 8, 17 n., 18, 20, 28, 32 and n., 42, 43, 47 and n., 48, 49, 55 and n., 59, 61, 64, 73, 75, 78, 79 n., 81, 86, 89, 106, 108, 118 and n., 130 n., 133 and n.

Arbuthnot, Robert, Dr. Arbuthnot's brother, 89 and n.

Arundel, Richard, M.P. for Knaresborough ?, 63.

Atheys or Atkeys, Mr., 1.

Attilio (Attilio Ariosti), composer, 43.

Ault, Norman, 29 n., 56 n., 96 n.

Avery, Emmett L., 134 n.

Ayre, William, 65 n.

Ballantyne, Archibald, 63 n.

Barber, John, Alderman, later Lord Mayor of London, 90.

Barber, Mary, Dublin poet, friend of Swift's, 106 and n., 109.

'Barnivelt, Esdras', 7 and n.

Barnstaple, Devon, Gay's birthplace, 1, 68 n.

Bartholomew Fair, 134 n.

Bartholomew Fair (Jonson), 53.

Bath, Somerset, 21, 39, 41, 42, 47, 72, 74, 75, 77 n., 78, 89, 93, 98, 108, 132.

Bath, William Pulteney, Earl of, *see* Pulteney, William.

Bathurst, Allen, Baron, later Earl, 43, 59, 72, 74, 77, 80, 87, 88, 90 and n., 104, 105, 123.

Batrachomuomachia, or The Battle of the Frogs and Mice (tr. Parnell), 17 n., 21, 26, 28, 29 and n.

Beattie, Dr. James, 48 n.

Bellenden, Mary, Maid of Honour, 33 and n., 37.

Berkeley, George, philosopher and Bishop of Cloyne, 41 and n., 50, 51 n., 123 and n.

Berkeley, James, 3rd Earl of, 55.

Bicknell or Bignell, Mrs., actress, 20.

Binfield, Berks., Pope's early home, 7 n., 11, 28–29.

Blackwell, Alfred E., 1 n.

Blount, Martha 'Patty', 26 n., 29, 33 n., 76, 108.

Blount, Teresa, 26 n.

Bolingbroke, Frances (Winchcombe) St. John, Lady, 72, 74, 75, 78, 123.

Bolingbroke, Henry St. John, Viscount, 3 n., 20, 41 n., 55, 56 n., 59 and n., 60, 72, 74, 78, 89, 117, 118 and n.

Bolton, Charles Paulet, 3rd Duke of, 76 and n.

Bononcini, Giovanni, composer, 43.

'Bookworm, The' (Parnell), 29 and n.

Bordoni, Faustina, singer, 52 and n.

Bounce, Pope's dog, 29, 96 n.

Bouzer, Mrs., Gay's landlady, 25 and n.

Bowry, Pope's waterman, 65 and n.

Boyce, Benjamin, 18 n.

PRINTED IN GREAT BRITAIN
AT THE UNIVERSITY PRESS, OXFORD
BY VIVIAN RIDLER
PRINTER TO THE UNIVERSITY